Lively Mac (J.H. MacOwen) teazing in the 1930s. (Doc Rowe Collection)

The Old Oss party at the Albert Hall for the International Folk Dance Festival, 1951.
Tom Gregor in top hat, Charlie Bate extreme left, (Col. Bate in the Oss.)
(Doc Rowe Collection)

The Old Oss at Prideaux Place, 1972. 'Colonel' Walter Bate sitting left, by Mr & Mrs Prideaux-Brune. (Photo: Doc Rowe)

PADSTOW'S OBBY OSS

AND MAY DAY FESTIVITIES

A STUDY
IN
FOLK LORE
AND
TRADITION
BY

Donald R. Rawe

LODENEK PRESS
PADSTOW

PADSTOW MAY SONGS.

THE MORNING SONG.

UNITE and unite and let us all unite,
  For summer is acome unto day,
And whither we are going we all will unite,
  In the merry morning of May.

I warn you young men every one,
  For summer is acome unto day,
To go to the green-wood and fetch your May home,
  In the merry morning of May.

Arise up Mr.—and joy you betide,
  For summer is acome unto day,
And bright is your bride that lies by your side,
  In the merry morning of May.

Arise up Mrs.—and gold be your ring,
  For summer is acome unto day,
And give to us a cup of ale the merrier we shall sing,
  In the merry morning of May.

  With the merry singing and the joy's a springing,
  For summer is acome unto day,
  How happy is the little bird that merrily doth sing.
  In the merry morning of May.

      (Repeated every four verses.)

Arise up Mr.—with your sword by your side,
  For summer is acome unto day,
Your steed is in the stable awaiting for to ride,
  In the merry morning of May.

Arise up Mr.—and reach me your hand,
  For summer is acome unto day,
And you shall have a lively lass with a thousand pounds in hand
  In the merry morning of May.

Arise up Mr.—I know you well afine,
  For summer is acome unto day.
You have a shilling in your purse and I wish it was in mine,
  In the merry morning of May.

Arise up Miss—and strew all your flowers,
  For summer is acome unto day,
It is but a while ago since we have strewed ours,
  In the merry morning of May.

Arise up Miss—all in your gown of green,
  For summer is acome unto day,
You are as fine a lady as wait upon the queen,
  In the merry morning of May.

Arise up Miss—out of your bed,
  For summer is acome unto day,
Your chamber shall be strewed with the white rose and the red,
  In the merry morning of May.

Arise up Miss—all in your smock of silk,
  For summer is acome unto day,
And all your body under as white as any milk,
  In the merry morning of May.

Where are the young men that here now should dance,
  For summer is acome unto day,
Some they are in England and some they are in France,
  In the merry morning of May.

Where are the maidens that here now should sing,
  For summer is acome unto day,
They are in the meadows the flowers gathering,
  In the merry morning of May.

The young men of Padstow might if they would,
  For summer is acome unto day,
They might have built a ship and gilded her with gold,
  In the merry morning of May.

The maidens of Padstow might if they would,
  For summer is acome unto day
They have made a garland and gilded it with gold,
  In the merry morning of May

Now fare you well, and we bid you good cheer,
  For the summer is acome unto day,
We will come no more unto your house before another year,
  In the merry morning of May.

THE DAY SONG.

AWAKE St. George, our English knight O,
  For summer is acome O, and winter is ago,
  And every day God give us his grace,
  By day and by night O.

Where is St. George, where is he O,
He is out in his long boat all on the salt sea O,
And in every land O, the land that ere we go.

  And for to fetch the summer home, the summer and the May O,
  For summer is acome O, and winter is ago.

Where are the French dogs, that make such boast O,
  They shall eat the grey goose feather,
And we will eat the roast O,
  And in every land O, the land that ere we go.

Thou might'st have shewn thy knavish face,
  Thou might'st have tarried at home O,
But thou shalt be an old cuckold,
  And thou shalt wear the horns.

  With Hal-an-tow, and joly rumble O,
  For summer is acome O, and winter is ago,
  And in every land O, the land that ere we go.

Up flies the Kite and down falls the Lark O,
  Aunt Ursula Birdhood she had an old ewe,
And she died in her own Park O.

  And for to fetch the summer home, &c.

  The Choruses to be repeated alternately.

PUBLISHED AND SOLD BY M. HARDING, STATIONER, ETC., PADSTOW.

(Reproduced from a broadsheet sold in Padstow about 1895)

A Blue Ribbon Oss before 1914.
Walter 'Colonel' Bate with triangle. Wm. 'Bluey' England on right.

'Peace Oss' (Blue Ribbon) late 1930's.
W.H. Thomas as May Lady.

The two Osses in the Market, Padstow about 1952.

Blue Ribbon Oss at Obby Oss Slipway, 1949.
Note Teazer's mask

Introduction

So much has been written, and recorded on film and sound-track, about the Padstow Obby Oss and its history, that it seems remarkable that until now no attempt has been made to issue a detailed account of it for popular reading.

In one way Padstow may count itself fortunate that no speculative publication written with an eye to tourists consumption and perpetuating the dubious myths with few of the hard historical facts, has appeared. Such a book would have been only too easy to produce and would have served us all ill, placing our Obby Oss and its followers in the realms of whimsy and quaint buffoonery: to which indeed, over a number of years (as the writings of historians and reporters attest) it was once consigned, and from which it has since been rescued.

The rescuers were men and women of devotion to true folklore and possessed of the scientific spirit of enquiry: Baring-Gould, Cecil Sharp, Thurstan Peter, Miss Banks and Miss Alford, to quote only some of them. Without their visits to Padstow and their painstaking efforts to record and evaluate our festivities and May Song, causing Padstonians themselves to realise the true value of their ancient custom, we should by now have been regarded as a town of mere frenzied idiocy, on that one day of the year which we all hold most dear.

What May Day means to us is a subject often expatiated upon by writers, both local and from 'abroad'. My intention here has been to avoid, as much as possible, all nostalgia and sentimentality; to record the facts as they are or were; to give all possible interpretations in an undogmatic fashion so that the reader may decide for himself about every aspect of the proceedings.

What has emerged from the fascinating 'goose chase' undergone for the research necessary to produce this work, is a picture of a town which, like Minehead, Helston and a few other places, has held on to its own peculiar form of welcoming in the summer, long after the custom died out elsewhere in Europe. Neither our Oss nor our May Song, may be quite as unique as we have fondly imagined them to be. But the indisputable fact remains that nowhere else are the festivities so vigorous, colourful and all-embracing; drawing in Padstonian and visitor, adult and child, layman and folklorist alike. When other places ignored or scorned May rites as something outworn and incomprehensible, Padstow held on to its May Day with a fierce undeterred love, and has made of it something eminently alive and significant for people everywhere who love to dance and sing.

My gratitude for help in compiling this book goes out to many people and institutions, in Padstow and outside. I wish particularly to mention the following: Mr. W.H. Thomas, for personal recollections and material lent; Messrs Walter and Ernest Bate, for the Old Oss; Mr. A.M. Brenton, Mrs. F. Buckingham, Mrs. M. O'Keefe, Mr. D. Farquhar, Mr. P. O'Keefe, jun., Mrs. M. Broadbent, for recollections and material; Mr. H.L. Douch and the staff of the County Museum, Truro, for assistance and kind permission to reproduce material from the Journal of the Royal Institution of Cornwall; Mr. David Bland, librarian of the Vaughan Williams Memorial Library at Cecil Sharp House, London, for generous help with research; the staff of Cornwall County Library; Messrs. Reg Hall and Christopher Ridley for material provided; Mr. J.J. Ruff of Trevone, for photographs; Mrs. M. Prior for unstinting help with typing, research and proof-reading; and the late Mr. Thomas Henry Williams for recollections, and material: a devoted Padstonian and indefatigable Mayer, to whose memory this book is affectionately dedicated.

Donald R. Rawe
(Scryfer Lanwednok)

March 1971

1. MAY DAY AT PADSTOW TODAY

At the present time, well into the latter half of the 20th century, Padstow Obby Oss and its May Day Festivities are recognised all over the world as a unique and living folk event, and each year some thousands of people come to see it. Padstow people from all over the world come home for the Great Day. It was not always so. Among other things this book sets out to show how the ancient custom developed from a quaint occurrence, carried on by a few devotees and hardly worth a mention in the works of writers on Cornwall, to the impressive and widely publicised spectacle it is today. Another purpose is to set down the true form of the Ossing so that it shall not, like so much else change or be lost to sight under pressure of the public attention it now receives.

Preparations

The men of the town begin preparations several days before, putting strings of flags across the main streets of the town, and bringing in greenery - the traditional sycamore branches - to decorate doorways, lamposts etc. The May Pole is set up in Broad Street, which has been its site since after the first world war. Other preparations - the repainting and repairing of the respective Osses - have already been attended to. A recent development has been a tendency, sometimes as early as a fortnight before May Day, for a crowd to assemble after the public houses close at night and to dance and sing (without the Oss) around the quayside and market place, until after midnight. This certainly causes some nuisance to those who live in that area of Padstow, but it should be remembered that this is, in effect, the main means of practising for May Day, and that without it much of the song might be lost. Already over the years several verses have disappeared from popular recollection and no one wishes to see this process continued. The May Day Festivities are, indeed, so full of spontaneous joy, and the May Tune is so vigorous and dance-inspiring, that it is difficult to blame those who express their anticipation of the summer and the May-O in this manner; although there are people who hold that the May Song, like the Oss himself, should not be brought into use until the Day itself.

Morning Song

The procedure today is that about a quarter to twelve on the eve of May Day the singers assemble outside the Golden Lion, home of the Old Oss, and await the striking of midnight. As the last notes of the church bell fade away they strike up the first verse of the Morning Song - 'Unite and Unite, and let us all unite'. They sing to the landlord and landlady of the Lion:

> Rise up, Mr. Hawken, and joy to you betide,
> For summer is acome unto day,
> And bright is your bride that lies down by your side,
> In the merry morning of May.

After the other verses they move off, to sing in Church Lane, Ruthy's Lane, Church Street, outside Prideaux Place; down High Street, along St. Saviour's Lane, through Oak Terrace and down the steps to Duke Street; and thereafter wherever the fancy takes them, usually until about 2.0 a.m. The general intention is to sing to various personalities of the town, not forgetting the   and bedridden, the appropriate verse according to their standing and situation. Thus to anyone reasonably prosperous:

> You have a shilling in your purse and I wish
> it was in mine...

And to a spinster, or the squire's lady:

> Rise up Miss (Mrs.) Brune, all in your gown of green..
> You are as fine a lady as waits upon the Queen.....

To a young beauty of the town:

> Rise up Miss ----, all in your smock of silk...
> And all your body under as white as any milk...

This night-singing has a special quality of its own; without drums, accordions or Oss, is creates a powerful folk-atmosphere and is one of the experiences of May Day that should not be missed. Part of the attraction is, of course, singing in darkness; not long ago a television company attempted to film it, every so often lighting flares for illumination, and considerably detracted from this part of the proceedings.

Day Festivities

The Blue Ribbon Oss is first to make its appearance, nowadays from the Institute steps, at 10.0 a.m. The Old Oss appears from its immemorial home, the Golden Lion Inn, at 11.0 a.m. Present day broadsheets (see p. 6) Give the Day Song as starting 'Unite and Unite', a verse identical to the Morning Song, and continuing 'All out of your beds, etc.' However, the 1903 broadsheet gives all sixteen verses (plus chorus, sung every four verses, 'With the Merry Ring...') as the Morning Song, and (see p. 7) the Day Song as an extended version of the 'slow' verses now printed as an interlude in italics - 'O Where is St. George, etc.' These verses actually fell out of use in the 1890's. This is an instance of the still-evolving pattern of the festivities: it is certain that in 1903 the Morning Song was sung during the day and was not simply reserved for the night singing. So the pattern is basically the same today: after a number of verses of the Morning Song, with its vigorous drumming and full accompaniment of accordions, during which the Oss prances and is 'teazed' in the fashion of a duel (which one might almost compare to bull or bear-baiting) a grave pause ensues, the Oss sinks down; the Teazer lays a doleful club on the canvas and the slow verse of the Day Song 'O Where is St. George...' is sung. It is a solemn moment, a dramatic pause before the sudden beat of the drums brings the Oss, and everyone back to joyful life:

With the merry ring, adieu the joyful spring...

The two Osses, by mutual consent, then visit various parts of the town without crossing each other's paths until the evening, when they meet around the Maypole. Their itineraries vary, but generally follow these forms:-

	Old Oss		Blue Ribbon Oss
Morning:	Golden Lion (11 a.m) Church Lane Ruthy's Lane Church Street Prideaux Place Duke Street Middle Street Golden Lion	Morning:	The Institute (10 a.m.) South Quay Station Road St Edmund's Lane Dennis Road Allan Road Annethy Lowen Trelawney Road
Afternoon:	Golden Lion (2 p.m.) Lanadwell Street Market Street South Quay Harbour Inn Metropole Dennis Road Sarah's Lane Lodenek Avenue Glynn Road Caswarth Terrace Social Club New Street Broad Street Golden Lion - Tea		Glynn Road Caswarth Terrace Social Club New Street Market Street Institute - Lunch
		Afternoon:	Market Street (2.30pm) Lanadwell Street Church Lane Ruthy's Lane Church Street Cross Street High Street Prideaux Place Church Street Duke Street Market Street Institute - Tea
Evening:	(6 p.m.) Perambulations around Lower Town, Quay and Maypole - route varies. Both Osses usually meet at this time. Golden Lion - Farewell	Evening:	(6 p.m.) Market Street North Quay South Quay Broad Street - Maypole (route varies) 9-10 p.m. Market Street - Farewell

Dress

The general dress of the Mayer is white ducks or jeans; white shirts, either blue or red ribbon worn as sash and belt; white sailors' caps with flowers (cowslips, bluebells, or tulips) affixed to them. The Old Oss party wear red and white spotted neckerchiefs. Each party is led by a Master of Ceremonies, dressed in a morning suit and top hat. This has become traditional and compares with the Helston Furry Dance. Until recently, a man dressed as a woman was part of the ensemble of the Blue Ribbon Oss, and before that of the Old Oss party. Today the Teazer wears no mask, but as we shall see ('Backalong') formerly various masks were worn and added greatly to the scene.

Collections

Both teams make collections from the onlookers. The Blue Ribbon Ossers collect for charity (generally for a local appeal fund, or coal for old folks at Christmas). This being their professed aim, no personal profit from the proceedings is taken by any member of the party. The Old Ossers stick doggedly to 'immemorial tradition', sharing profits amongst themselves for their enjoyment after all expenses have been paid. However it has become established that after May Day the Old Oss party disguise themselves in various costumes and sing 'darky' songs in the tradition of the Nigger Minstrels, and parade through the town, paying special attention to the inns, collecting for the local branch of the Red Cross. They have collected some hundreds of pounds in this way.

Ossing as Folklore

What draws many people to visit Padstow at this time of year is the place Padstow's festivities, and particularly the Obby Oss, has in folklore. Today May 1st is celebrated by various activities all over the world, some political and some pastoral, but in the later Middle Ages it was the great day of Summer's coming, one of the main festivals of the year, more important then than Christmas: to be welcomed by dances and songs of one kind or another, all over Britain

Combined teams with Old Oss at Prideaux Place, 1944. J.H. MacOwen (in white pullover) and William England (with Brenton drum). T.C. Gregor in top hat. W. Bate at back next to Mr. Brune.

The Old Oss, about 1910
(W.H. Baker & Dasher Revely in foreground)

and Europe. Now only Padstow, with one or two other places, keeps up the thorough-going May Day celebrations. Padstow's festivities are certainly unique in the form and expression they take: nowhere else is found such a powerful May Song, nowhere else such a vigorous, if at times terrifying, hobby horse. More of the history of the hobby later: for now it is sufficient to recall that a very few examples still survive elsewhere, in debased form, whereas once hobby horses could be found, usually associated with Morris Dances, all over Britain. So when the Padstow Obby Oss appears at Festivals of the English Folk Dance and Song Societies held at the Royal Albert Hall in London, often in an international programme, it is the star of the occasion, the climax of the programme. No one who has seen it, appearing among the other folk-events of Britain and Europe, can fail to realise its importance.

The Revels as Drama

Serious students of drama now visit Padstow to enquire into the origins and significance of the Oss and festivities. For it is recognised that this duel between Oss and Teazer, the spontaneous dancing and complex (if obscure) story of the May Song, is a fine example of the earliest and most basic form of drama: the folk festival. Everyone can join in, whether Padstonians or 'foreigners' provided they are sufficiently adept at picking up the words and tune. This is audience-involvement at its best, free, jubilant, welcoming all with open arms. The mime of Oss and Teazer has a wealth of significance for those who seek meanings: the duel of winter and summer, of St. George (or was it St. Petroc?) and the Dragon, of Christian and Devil; of seed sower and Corn Spirit. (See Origins section of this book.) It matters little which interpretation one favours: the drama lives, draws the spectator, sets his feet tapping and then dancing, then his throat singing before he knows it.

May Day as Spectacle

Of recent years, particularly since the advent of television into most people's homes, the Ossing has been presented to millions of people as a unique, quaint and slightly mad revel which has nothing whatever to do with the 20th century: the quality of attraction portrayed is usually an escapist one, drawing those who wish to forget the drab complexities of the modern world and escape into the simpler, romantic past. But despite the numbers of visitors, some three or four thousand each May Day and increasing every year, by and large the Oss teams pay little attention to this publicity, and to their great credit get on with the festivities in their full-blooded unspoiled fashion. Romanticism seems out of place when confronted with the scarifying monster, the thump of the Brenton drum into the listener's stomach; and the man carrying the Oss, all 100 lb. of him, hardly feels he is indulging in a sentimental revival of a quaint old custom.

In his book 'Cornwall', Claude Berry, a Padstonian and Editor of the West Briton, wrote:-

> We at Padstow are quite unself-conscious and informal in our festivity. Anybody and everybody can join in. Well we know that crowds will not come from elsewhere to watch our revels; and we are neither sad nor glad therefor. Ours is not a "show piece" to be staged with elegance and precision for the satisfaction of the formal or the delectation of strangers.

That was written in 1949. Today the picture is vastly different. Indeed some senior mayers complain that the crowds of visitors restrict the dancing: in Claude Berry's day the crowd could still keep to the street sides and pavements and allow the Oss plenty of room. But the dancing is as energetic as ever, the forays into the crowd (where space permits flight) still effective.

Blue Ribbon Oss. Trethillick Lane about 1902.

5

2. THE MAY SONG: THEN AND NOW

<u>The Words:</u>

The present-day form of the two songs (Morning, or Night Song, and the Day Song) as set out in the 'Original Obby Oss' party's leaflet, differs from that of the earlier versions dating from 1903 and before. This is the song as sung today:

NIGHT SONG

Unite and unite and let us all unite,
   For summer is acome unto day,
And whither we are going we will all unite,
   In the merry morning of May.

I warn you young men everyone
   For summer is acome unto day,
To go to the green-wood and fetch your May home
   In the merry morning of May.

Arise up Mr. ...... and joy you betide,
   For summer is acome unto day,
And bright is your bride that lies by your side,
   In the merry morning of May.

Arise up Mrs. ...... and gold be your ring,
   For summer is acome unto day,
And give to us a cup of ale the merrier we shall sing,
   In the merry morning of May.

Arise up Miss ...... all in your gown of green,
   For summer is acome unto day,
You are as fine a lady as wait upon the Queen,
   In the merry morning of May.

Now fare you well, and we bid you all good cheer,
   For summer is acome unto day,
We call once more unto your house before another year,
   In the merry morning of May.

DAY SONG

Unite and unite and let us all unite,
   For summer is acome unto day,
And whither we are going we will all unite,
   In the merry morning of May.

Arise up Mr. ...... I know you well afine,
   For summer is acome unto day,
You have a shilling in your purse and I wish it were in mine,
   In the merry morning of May.

All out of your beds,
   For summer is acome unto day,
Your chamber shall be strewed with the white rose and the red
   In the merry morning of May.

Where are the young men that here now should dance,
   For summer is acome unto day,
Some they are in England some they are in France,
   In the merry morning of May.

Where are the maidens that here now should sing
   For summer is acome unto day,
They are in the meadows the flowers gathering,
   In the merry morning of May.

Arise up Mr. ...... with your sword by your side,
   For summer is acome unto day,
Your steed is in the stable awaiting for to ride,
   In the merry morning of May.

Arise up Miss ...... and strew all your flowers,
   For summer is acome unto day,
It is but a while ago since we have strewed ours,
   In the merry morning of May.

   O! where is St. George,
   O, where is he O?
   He is out in his long boat on the salt sea O.
   Up flies the kite and down falls the lark O.
   Aunt Ursula Birdhood she had an old ewe
   And she died in her own Park O.

With the merry ring, adieu the merry spring,
   For summer is acome unto day,
How happy is the little bird that merrily doth sing,
   In the merry morning of May.

The young men of Padstow they might if they would,
   For summer is acome unto day,
They might have built a ship and gilded her with gold,
   In the merry morning of May.

The young women of Padstow might if they would,
   For summer is acome unto day,
They might have made a garland with the white rose
     and the red,
   In the merry morning of May.

Arise up Mr. ...... and reach me your hand,
   For summer is acome unto day,
And you shall have a lively lass with a thousand pounds
     in hand,
   In the merry morning of May.

Arise up Miss ...... all in your cloak of silk
   For summer is acome unto day,
And all your body under as white as any milk,
   In the merry morning of May.

   O! where is St. George, O where is he O? etc.
   With the merry ring, adieu the merry spring, etc.

Now fare you well and bid you all good cheer,
   For summer is acome unto day,
We call no more unto your house before another year,
   In the merry morning of May.

The Blue Ribbon Team's leaflet has a shorter first song (entitled Morning Song); and two verses of the Old Team's Day Song do not appear in their version: 'Where are the maidens that here now should sing' and 'Arise up Miss .... all in your cloak of silk'.

But the most remarkable change that has taken place in the May Song during the last hundred years is that most of the former Day Song has been left out, and that what used to be known as the Morning Song is now regarded as the Day Song.

The original 'Day Song' was as follows:

Awake, St. George, our English knight O,
   For summer is acome O and winter is a-go,
And every day God give us his grace,
   By day and night O.
Where is St. George, where is he O,
   He is out in his long-boat all on the salt sea O,
And in every land O, the land that ere we go.

(1st Chorus)
And for to fetch the summer home, the summer and the May O,
For summer is acome O, and winter is a-go.

Where are the French dogs that make such boast O,
   They shall eat the grey goose feather,
And we will eat the roast O,
   And in every land O, the land that ere we go.

Thou might'st have shown they knavish face,
   Thou might'st have tarried at home O,
But thou shalt be an old cuckold,
   And thou shalt wear the horns.

(2nd Chorus)
With Hal-an-tow and jolly rumble O
For summer is acome O, and winter is a-go,
And in every land O, the land that ere we go.

Up flies the kite and down falls the Lark O,
   Aunt Ursula Birdhood she had an old ewe
And she died in her own Park O,

And for to fetch the summer home, etc.

It will be seen that this whole song has become attenuated into two verses, 'O Where is St. George ...' and 'Up Flies the Kite...' These have now become a chorus or interlude in the main May Song. Whether this is an improvement or not is hard to say; it may well be, viewed dramatically and symbolically, since the short but most effective 'dying' and 'reviving' of the Oss is one of the dance's salient and most impressive features. We may assume that this was traditionally a part of the proceedings, symbolising the death of winter and coming of summer. However, as we are told by Hitchens and Drew (p.16) that this 'dirge' was sung by the Oss party on taking the Oss out to Treator Pool, we may well ask at what point in those days did the dying and revival take place. As far as can be gathered from the memories of those still living, the full Day Song ceased to be used in the 1890's. How did they march or dance, out to Treator, whilst singing this full version? It seems we shall never know, since no record has been made. The song is a slow march, certainly. Did the Oss, on reaching the Pool, sink down and dip his snappers into the water, as the St. George verse was sung? This would presumably have been the appropriate juncture for the act; but those who can remember taking the Oss out to the Pool tend to think that the dipping was not done during the song at all, but was a culminating silent part of the proceedings.

Earlier versions of the Songs

Hitchens and Drew in 1824 recorded two verses of the Day Song (see p.16). The first full version to be published was by Henry Boase, in the Western Antiquary of June 1887, and a few years later Baring-Gould's first, and rather faulty version, was published in the London Illustrated News. During the 1890's Henry Harding, stationer, of Padstow, issued a large broadsheet with the full song, which is reproduced on the back cover of this book. This may be taken to be the authoritative rendering used at the time, although (see preceding section) the full Day Song was even then in process of being abandoned. The following verses in Harding's sheet should be compared to those being sung today:

Unite and Unite and let us all unite
   For Summer is acome unto day,
And whither we are going we all will unite
   In the merry morning of May.

With the merry singing and the joy's a springing
   For Summer is acome unto day
How happy is the little bird that merrily doth sing
   In the merry morning of May.

Arise up Miss ... all in your smock of silk
   For Summer is acome unto day.
And all your body under as white as any milk,
   In the merry morning of May.

'Summer issy come unto day'. Thurstan Peter, in his address to the Royal Institution of Cornwall at Truro in 1913, regarded this as a corruption: ' "Summer is acome unto day" is no doubt "Summer is y-cumen today".' Inglis Gundry in his collection of Cornish Folk Songs, Canow Kernow adopts this interpretation and gives 'icumen today' in his version. He comments:

    The word "icumen", as in "Summer is icumen in", could easily be a survival from the later Middle Ages when the English language was first being spoken at Padstow, and this would remove all grounds for the rather pointless, though admittedly attractive, "unto day", which is shouted out so emphatically by the onlookers, thereby making inaudible the beautiful fall of the melody in bars 6 - 7.

Baring Gould took down the words and published them in his 'Garland of Country Song', 1895. An article he wrote for the London Illustrated News a few years prior (about 1889) to that gives what appears to be an earlier version still of the Day Song, which he calls 'The Hobby-Horse Song' to distinguish it from the song of the Hobby-Horse Pairs ('The May Night Song'):

Refrain: Awake, St. George, our English knight O !
For summer is a-come, and winter is ago.

1. Where is St. George? and where is he, O?
   He's down in his long boat upon the salt sea, O!

   Refrain: For to fetch summer home, the summer and May, O !
   The summer is a-come and winter is ago.

2. Where are the French dogs, that made such boast, O?
   They shall eat the goose-feather, and we'll eat the roast, O!

3. Thou should'st not ha' shown they knavish face, and tarried at home, O!
   But thou shalt be a rascal and shalt wear the horn, O!

4. Up flies the kite, down falls the lark, O!
   Aunt Ursula Birdwood, she had an old yeo.

5. Aunt Ursula Birdwood, she had an old yeo,
   And she died in her own park, long, long ago.

'Rascal' (verse 3), instead of 'cuckold' (see p. 7), is a clear instance of Baring Gould deliberately bowdlerising a folk song which he was collecting - a general practice with him. It is most likely that the differences between this c. 1889 version and later ones are due to sheer inaccuracy of reporting or transcribing in this early record.

Space does not permit, in this edition, to reproduce all the versions of the music which have been noted by musicologists, folklorists, etc., some published, some not. Reg Hall and Mervyn Plunkett give a comparison of R.H. Worth's version (1860, from Baring-Gould's Mss. in Plymouth Public Library) of the slow Day Song with the 'St. George' and 'Aunt Ursula' verses as sung today. They also record several Morning and Night Song variants. Baring-Gould and Fleetwood Sheppard's version (A Garland of Country Song) attempts, quite unjustifiably, to alternate verses of the Morning Song with verses of the former Day Song. Inglis Gundry's admirable collection, Canow Kernow, gives the song as recorded by B.H. Watts in 1860; by Baring Gould in 1891; by Thurstan Peter in 1912/13; by Cecil Sharp in 1914; by Edgar Tonkin, 1928 (this version was published in Dr. Ralph Dunstan's Cornish Song Book); and two versions, from the Red and the Blue teams respectively, collected by Gundry himself on May Day 1962. He also records a variation used by one of the colt oss teams, whose children's voices could not reach some of the deeper notes. Some extremely interesting descriptions and comments are also included. Here follows the music as recorded by Thurstan Peter in 1913, with a snatch of the forgotten version of the Day Song:

THE HOBBY HORSE

Padstow May (or Hobby Horse) Songs.

Morning Song.

THE HOBBY HORSE

Day Song (Cont^d.)

And in every land O. The land that e'er we go.

Verses of 3 lines finish at X

"Chorus."

mm ♩ = 70

And for to fetch home the Summer (or) the Summer and the Summer and the May Summer home O For Summer is a come O and Winter is ago.

The origin of the May Song tune, if it could be satisfactorily established, would doubtless throw considerable light upon the source and evolution of the whole festivity. It appears likely that Padstow's song has developed from the general Morris dance tunes brought to Britain during the 14th century or even earlier. Thurstan Peter was probably not the first to recognise the similarity between the May Song and Helston's Hal-an-Tow and Furry Dance tunes, so much so that in the Journal of R.I.C. of 1913 he printed the music to both. H. Fleetwood Sheppard thought that the song was one originally well-known all over England, and celebrated Henry V's victory at Agincourt (we know that a Cornish contingent marched into that battle under a banner showing two wrestlers in a 'hitch': were Padstow men among them?). But Reg Hall and Mervyn Plunkett go further: in their excellent article. 'May Day - Padstow' in their folk magazine Ethnic (now alas deceased) of Summer 1959 they state:

> Almost every known English May Song is a variant of this tune . . . the two tunes (i.e. Morning and Day, or dirge) are in fact different treatments of the same tune. This tune is not only 'standard' for May Songs but it is also known from wassailing songs and at least one New Year Carol, sung in Cuckfield, Sussex.

Thus in its very song Padstow is one of the last places to maintain a tradition which was at one time generally observed all over Britain and large areas of Europe.

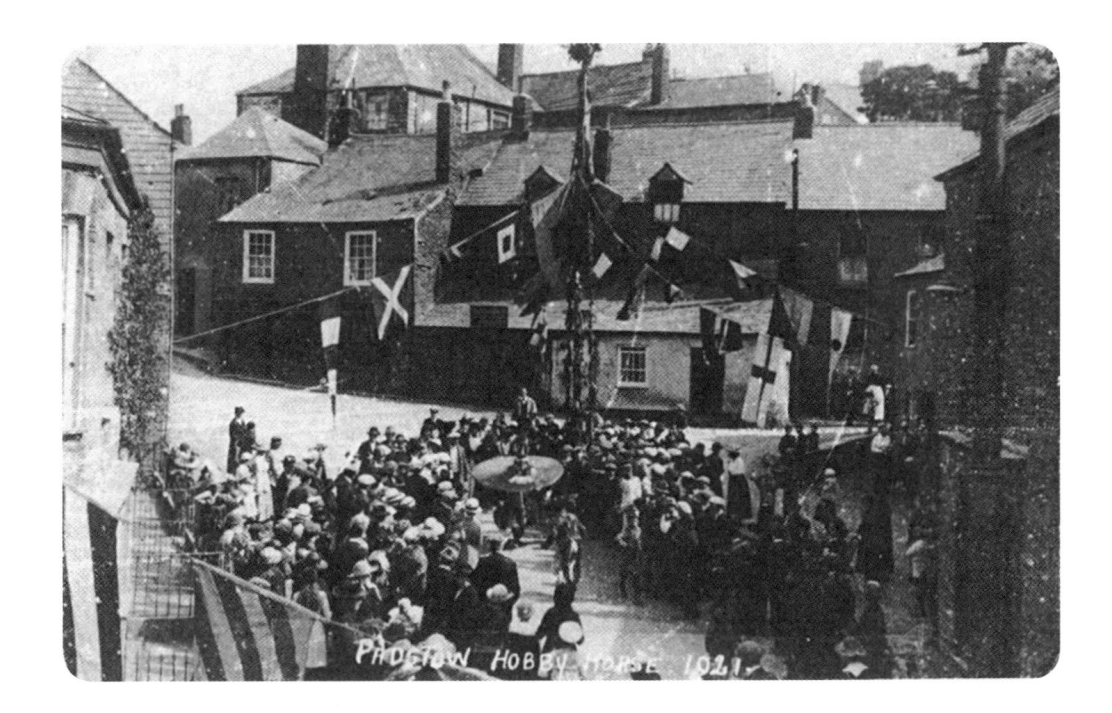

Scene in Broad Street, May Day 1921

3. ORIGINS OF THE OBBY OSS AND ITS RITES

In his 1913 lecture, Thurstan Peter, Cornish historian, antiquarian and editor of the Journal of the Royal Institution of Cornwall, pointed out that the 8th May was the old Celtic Bealtaine, or Beltane, when the coming in of summer was observed with the lighting of fires. May 1st had come to be bonfire day in Scotland and Ireland. It seems almost certain that, confused and later combined with the Morris may-games and celebrations which in the Middle Ages became popular all over Britain, this is the original source of the basic festivities themselves. Peter's comments in this connection are interesting:-

> I believe the (Padstow) Hobby Horse and the (Helston) Furry Dance alike to be ancient pagan festivals of revival and of fruitfulness, one of those forms of magic, not by any means implying the notion of invariable cause and effect, but an attempt to express in ritual the emotions and desires - and on to this have been grafted on the one hand folk-lore and on the other Christian ceremonies, the history being still further confused by mistaken efforts of well-meaning persons to remove elements regarded by them as coarse.

We can in fact find many rites of similar intent, not only in Great Britain but on the continent. Thurstan Peter says that until the early years of the 20th century,

> ... in West Cornwall ... it was the custom to hang a piece of furze over the door on the morning of May-Day; at Penzance the boys 'scare away the devil' by blowing horns, the discord of which ought to suffice for the purpose, and on May-Day the children gather green boughs which they indiscriminately call May; at Polperro, people went into the country on that day and brought home branches of the small-leaved Cornish elm or sprays of flowering white thorn (calling both by the same name of "May"), and occasionally exercised their cherished privilege of throwing into the water anyone not bearing a twig of one or other sacred tree, singing as they did so, "The first of May is dipping day". At Helston, the same treatment was meted out to those who worked on Furry Day. At Looe the boys dressed their hats with flowers, and carried bullocks' horns filled with water which they spirted over such as had no "May" about them.

Other examples of May customs can be found in Mary Courtney's Cornish Feasts and Folklore, Bottrell's Hearthside Traditions, Hunt's Drolls, and Hone's Every Day Book. Thurstan Peter noted that the Oss at Padstow makes his first appearance through an arch of sycamore, or May leaves, and, of course, the Mayer was and is always liberally garlanded with flowers. This is basically a religious rite, a fertility transference by which the wearer expects some power of the new blooms and leaves to pass into himself. So it is evident that May Day at Padstow was originally part of a country-wide festival for summer's coming.

Here the Morris traditions must be mentioned. The first documented reference to these May games and their characters is in the early 17th Century, but it is apparent that they had been customary all over Britain for some time - possibly two or three centuries - before that. Popular dances are said to have been acquired from the Moors, perhaps on the return of John of Gaunt from Spain in the reign of Edward III (reign from 1327-1377). The oldest recorded Morris tune is found in Arbeau's or Tabourot's Orchésographie, 1589. Morris (deriving from the Spanish 'morisco' = Moors) is said to be a reference to the early custom of the participants of blacking their faces in disguise. The integral elements of Morris are a May Pole, dancers, Robin Hood and Maid Marion, and - the Hobby Horse (Hobby = dim. Robin).

We know that a hobby horse custom existed in 18th and 19th Century West Cornwall. The creature was known as the Penglas: Miss B.C. Spooner, writing in Folk Lore (the Journal of the Folk Lore Society), 1958, said:

> 'The Hobby Horse that went with the Land's End Christmas Mummers not so long ago was that sort that consists of a horse's skull held up on a stick by a hide-covered or sheet-draped man, and had its own name in the Cornish Language: Pen-glas. Grey Head'.

The head may originally have been an actual horse-skull, but R. Edmonds (The Land's End District, 1862), describing the mechanics of the Penglas wrote:

> A piece of wood in the form of a horse's head and neck with contrivance for opening and shutting the mouth with a loud snapping noise ... covered with coarse cloth or hide.

Spooner considered the Penglas to have been similar in aspect and behaviour at that time, late 18th Century to 19th, to the Padstow Hobby Horse, especially as it captured girls under its skirts as part of a fertility rite. Miss M. Banks called it a 'true brother to the snapping biting beast of Padstow'. Since both Polwhele and C.S. Gilbert refer to the Padstow Oss as a man in a horse's skin, it is possible that around 1800 the two were rather similar; for, as we shall see (Backalong) at that time Padstow's Oss had not acquired its ferocious mask. On the other hand it is also possible that neither Polwhele nor Gilbert actually saw Padstow's Oss and that they <u>assumed</u> it was similar to the Penglas, its gown being of actual horse-hide. Further research alone, if possible, can <u>resolve</u> this question.

The earliest written reference to a hobby horse is actually in the old Cornish drama Bewnans Meriasek (The Life of Meriasek) written in 1502. This at least points to the conclusion that hobby horsing was general in Cornwall at the time:

		Translation by Dr. Whitley Stokes:	
	(descendit Teudarus)		(Teudar goes down)
Teudarus:	Yu hemma oll an confort	Teudar:	Is this all the consolation
	a'm bedha dyworthouth-why?		I am to have from you?
	Ay, Serys, yma dheugh sport		Eh, Sirs, you have sport
	pan us dughan dhymmo-vy.		when I have grief.
	Wel, wel, na fors!		Well, well, no matter!
	Re Appolyn, ow dew splan,		By Apollo, my glorious god,
	kens dyberth, ny wharth ma's ran:		before parting only some will laugh:
	me a be dhe 'n Hobyhors		I will pay out the Hobbyhorse
	ha'y gowetha!		and its pair!
	Hava that, peswar lorel!		Have that, you four idlers!
	hag arta pertheugh cof gwell		and another time remember better
	pandr' wrellen dheugh comondya.		what I command you.

Padstow Hobby Horse about 1830

Blue Ribbon Oss about 1903

The Hobby Horse here referred to would probably have been a Camborne district one, very similar to the Penglas. Other Horse Festivals survive, or survived long enough to be written about: relics of the Morris, not all of them held on May Day. The characters and the dances evolved were entertaining enough, in days when winter needed brightening with social activities, to become adopted on other occasions.

Sir Walter Scott in his novel 'The Abbott' (1820) describes the Hobby Horse festivities at Lochleven, Scotland:

> Here one fellow with a horse's head painted before him, and a tail behind, and the whole covered with a long foot-cloth, which was supposed to hide the body of the animal, ambled, caracoled, pranced and plunged, as he performed the celebrated part of the hobbie-horse, so often alluded to in our ancient drama.

A similar description of a hobby horse's 'frisking' is given in Hone's Every Day Book (1826), under May 1st. A list of known Horse Festivals includes the Hooden Horse of East Kent (at Christmas), the Mari Llwyd of Wales - a large berribboned skull-type head carried by a man in a white cloak - also at Christmas; the Minehead Hobby Horse (May Eve and for two days following); the Coombe Martin Hobby, on Ascension Day; and others in Cheshire, Yorkshire and King's County, Ireland. These are surveyed by Violet Alford in her paper, 'Some Hobby Horses of Great Britain'. Miss Alford also writes (Enc. Brit.) of others abroad:

> South Indian Hobby Horses attend weddings. Javanese Hobbies are of woven basketwork. All Europe possess examples, and North Germany a white hobby horse is said to be Wotan's steed. Those of Spain and Provence are ornate and processional. Great Britain boasts the Old Oss at Padstow, Cornwall, appearing on May Day to catch women, and the Minehead, Somerset, Horse which catches strangers. The Welsh Mari Llwyd appears on the Gower coast at midwinter; Ireland had a similar skull-type to attend the midsummer fires. Iberian influence took the hobby-horse to Latin America.

And there is, or was, the October Horse at Rome, representing the Corn Spirit (Jevons, Plutarch's Romane Questions).

<u>The Horse as a fertility symbol</u>

How did the Hobby Horse come to be associated with Morris and the May Games?

It should be remembered that before the days of mechanisation the horse was the all-important power supply of agriculture. Not only did he do most of the work on farms, but no ploughing was possible without him, once he had superseded oxen as a more efficient means. The stallion is an animal of immense virility, and old manuals quote the recommended figure of fifty mares to one stallion - a far higher proportion of females serviced by each male than is the case with other animals. These considerations link up with the following illuminating extract from Alan Harlow's article 'The May Rites':

> Probably the most well-known celebration of the ritual year, both here and in Europe, was May Day, now but a wasted shadow of its former glory as the foremost festival of the ceremonial calendar. Traditionally a day of hobby-horses and Robin Hood festivals, of round-dances and the symbolic May Pole (earlier a sacred tree or stone) all dating back to palaeolithic times, May Day marked the commencement of the agricultural year; the time when, in the old religions, the passing of winter was celebrated and offerings were made to fertility gods to propitiate the new growth. Houses were decorated with green boughs and the hobbys pranced their way through every village to induce fertility in both nature and man. In England these festivities took the form of the Old English May Games, which were condemned by the Church as a resurgence of uninhibited and licentious paganism. However, they survived in their more complete form until the Reformation (the Romish pre-reformation church, although never accepting the Games, were quite content to avert their eyes from such primitive lapses), when the Puritans, horrified at the orgiastic nature of the celebrations, soon introduced severe legislation to terminate such heresies.
>
> Originally the Games comprised four distinct parts: the choosing and ceremonial parade of the May King and Queen; the Morris dance performed by masked or otherwise disguised men bearing swords; the Hobby Horse and the Rob Hood.
>
> It should be noted here that this Hobby is not the semicomical hobby of the Morris dance which, of late, it has become confused with, but a wild horse, a black demon cum vegetation spirit and the symbol of male fertility. Strangely enough, from time out of mind, black has always been associated with rites of fertility. All ritual horses are black and, up to a few years ago, used to shower and smear with soot any young maiden they could catch. In ancient Greece, black calves and sheep were always sacrificed to the fertility Goddess Demeter, who was portrayed as being half horse. It is still considered "lucky" to touch or shake hands with a sweep. Of the ritual horses at Padstow and elsewhere, Violet Alford writes - "All the animals are of the magical sort. They represent a wild not a domestic horse; they snap, they bite, they seize devotees; some die or fall to pieces; all are closely bound up with the fertility of the earth and of humankind, made of bits of plough, sieves, corn, maize; they undergo rain charms." The same is the black stallion that gave rise to the "Poor Old Horse" in its many variants, that was traditionally sung in connection with the ritual commemorating the death of the old year on All Hallows' Tide and the beginning of the new on All Souls' Day. Here, as in the Soul-Cakers Play from the Guilden Sutton (a Cheshire variant of the Mummers), he clearly represents the fertility god, dead for the duration of the winter. In this light, an additional aspect is added to his appearance in the May Games - that of resurrection.

Harlow goes on to trace the descent of the Morris dancers from the sorcerers of the palaeolithic age, as seen in stone-age cave paintings, and quotes the fact that ribbons and garters were brought in as evidence (for the prosecution) in 16th and 17th century trials for witchcraft. Even in those relatively late times organised Christianity was still trying to drive out and discredit the old pagan and Druid religion, which had lingered on all over Britain for so long, debased and half forgotten but still treasured among the common people. For a time the Puritans of the Commonwealth banished Morris Dances and Hobby Horses, though they reappeared in some places with the Restoration. (For a detailed description of the May Games see Hone's Every Day Book, under the entry for May 1st).

In the 4th Century A.D. the great St. Augustine preached against horse-magic: 'If you ever hear of anyone carrying out that most filthy practice of dressing up like a horse or a stag, chastise him most severely'. In the 7th Century, St. Adhelm also referred to them with disapproval. (Lach-Szyrma, Western Antiquary, 1890). In Bulgaria, where hobby horse customs are still taken most seriously, to the extent of invading rural villages and fighting with other 'horses' sometimes to death, a young man was solemnly warned by his priest that if he died inside his horse-costume he could not be buried in consecrated ground. (A.L. Lloyd, quoted by V. Alford, 1968). These instances should be sufficient evidence of the war waged by the Christian churches against what they regard as evil and pagan customs.

It would seem feasible to relate the Padstow May Pole to the sacred stone around which the pre-Celtic people of the district danced and upon which they offered sacrifices. The observation about 'resurrection' is certainly striking in view of the Obby Oss's dying and reviving ritual - something which no other British Hobby Horse ceremony seems to have retained. Douglas Neil Kennedy, President of the Folk Lore Society, writing of the Morris tradition in the Encyclopaedia Brittanica, comments that dances of a similar nature have survived among the Basques in France, in Spain,

Portugal, the Balkans and South America, and that their common feature is of a group of men attending on a pagan god (usually an animal-man of some kind) who celebrates his revival after death.

Not long ago young women pursued and captured by the Oss were marked by soot or blacking off the canvas of the creature (see Claude Berry, 'Cornwall', p. 181/2). George Boase, in the Western Antiquary of June 1887 wrote that people called on by the Padstow Obby Oss party in 1880 were greeted by showers of soot, and that the inside of the gown was smeared with blacklead to mark the 'victims' the Oss captured. As for rain charms - the invoking of the supernatural to bring rains and swell the corn - the former 'drinking' of the Oss at Treator Pool, and immersion in the quay waters, and the sprinkling of bystanders with the water (see Backalong, Polwhele, C.S. Gilbert, Hitchins and Drew), are surely evidence enough, though the actual meaning of this part of the ceremony had long been forgotten among Ossers before they discarded it. It seems evident that the 'sprinkling' had degenerated into mere horse-play.

Thurstan Peter quotes F.B. Jevons' Plutarch's "Romane Questions", 1892:

> The fructifying power of the spirit is supposed in modern folk-lore and in Africa, as it was at Rome, to reside specially in the animal's tail, which therefore was preserved over the hearth of the King's house in order to secure a good harvest next year.

The significance of the tail seems to have been lost at Padstow (though a small tail of real horsehair is still to be seen on the Oss), but it undoubtedly survived in a debased form at Minehead until the early 1900's. H.W. Kille, of Minehead, wrote in a booklet on his local hobby horse:

> ... a cow's tail was spliced to the end of the rope. As the man carrying the horse prances and gambles about, he occasionally swings the tail with much vigour to the danger of any unsuspecting bystander who happens to be within its reach.

This practice with a real cow's tail has recently been revived at Minehead.

St. Petroc and the Dragon

Other interpretations of the significance of Padstow Oss are possible. Canon Doble, writing his great work on the lives of Cornish Saints, included in his account of St. Petroc Mr. Athelstan Riley's theory of the origin of the Obby Oss. One of the most prominent legends of St. Petroc, featured in his life written by the monks of Bodmin, is that he banished a certain fearsome dragon, which had been terrorising the Padstow district, by binding it with his girdle and leading it to the sea where it swam away. Mr. Riley, an antiquarian, of Little Petherick, suggested that this is the origin of the Oss, which represents the Dragon, and of the Teazer, representing the Saint. He pointed out that immersing the Oss in the water of the harbour was formerly part of the May Day ritual (one of our slipways is still known to the older generations as 'Obby Oss Slip'), as was the visit to Treator, where in Mr. Riley's time there existed a large pond known as Treator pool, where the Oss was brought to drink. Searching for the swamp which the dragon used as his lair. Mr. Riley thought it most likely that in St. Petroc's time this area, still in our day well-wooded, could have been a veritable tangle of thicket and mud. This is a fascinating hypothesis: the only thing it lacks is evidence that around 520-540 A.D. reptiles of the requisite size and strength existed in Britain. (This was said to be the last Cornish dragon, which in its cannibalistic fashion had eaten up the others of its kind, introduced by the tyrant Teudar, Prince of Meneage: who is a character in Bewnans Meriasek, as we have seen). The event happened, it would seem, about the same time of year as the Beltane celebrations, and it is possible that a commemoration of St. Petroc's deed became part of the traditional welcoming in of summer; later to be confused with St. George and the Dragon and the Hobby Horse of the Morris. Thus, according to this theory, when we sing:

O where is St. George, O where is he O ?
He's out in his long boat, All on the salt sea O . . .

we are actually referring to St. Petroc's heroic feat with the last Cornish dragon.

Aunt Ursula and the French

A persistent story, often accepted as an explanation of the origin of the Oss, is that of Aunt Ursula Birdhood and the Frightening of the French. It is said that during one of the wars against France the men at Padstow being away to the wars, a French man o'war appeared off Stepper Point. Under Aunt Ursula's directions, the women, nothing daunted, wrapped themselves in their best red Sunday cloaks and marched, with the Oss at their head, out along the cliffs, with drums beating in support. The French sailors, seeing this 'army' in the distance with what they took to be the Devil at their head, upped anchor and sailed away. Mr. Francis Docton, a tailor of Padstow, informed one of his workmen (who was still living in Thurstan Peter's day) that the Hobby Horse first appeared at Padstow during the Siege of Calais (1346/7) and scared off the French in the aforesaid manner. The men of Padstow, said Mr. Docton, had gone to the Siege in two ships built by them. (This latter is a fact substantiated by historical evidence.) Mr. T.H. Williams was sceptical. Would the women have have risked being shot at by a ship's cannon, and in any case, if this was so effective, why had Padstow not scared off the Vikings in this manner, who sacked the town in 981 A.D. ? Polwhele (1803) also dismisses this story, with some contempt.

Nevertheless, in this connection the significance of this verse should be contemplated:

> Where are the young men that here should dance ......
> Some they are in England and some they are in France ......

which convincingly suggests that all the young men were away fighting the French when the man o'war appeared.

Also Where are the French dogs that here should boast O
They shall eat the grey goose feather and we shall eat the roast O!

seems to be a triumphant reference to the 'victory' won by the women of Padstow. The earliest published version, Hitchens and Drew, 1824, has "Where are the French dogs - they are on the coast O" - which is even more specific a reference.

It is interesting that similar stories of using a Hobby Horse to warn of invaders have been noted down at other places along the Irish Sea and Bristol Channel, particularly at Minehead and Fishguard. At Minehead, they say, the Danes were the would-be invaders. Whether we give credence to the story or not matters little. It is an exciting addition to the lore of the Oss, and as Aunt Ursula herself appears in the Day Song, her yowe or ewe dying peacefully in her own parc (Cornish, Field), instead of being roasted for the invaders' feasting, it does at least give the song and dance a further significance; without meaning, folk customs soon die out. The Birdhoods, incidentally, were a well-known Cornish family of standing during several centuries: at Lelissick Farm, Padstow, is a field named on the Tithe Map 'Park-O' field.

The Minehead Horse

A comparison of the Padstow Oss with the Minehead Hobby reveals some significant facts. There is no actual May Song at Minehead; the followers of the horse sing whatever songs they please, traditional or modern, but they play a tune referred to as the Hobby Horse Tune which is actually an old air entitled Soldier's Joy. May Day Eve is known as 'Warning Eve' - the meaning of 'warn' in this connection seems to be in the nature of 'giving notice' that the festivity is about to commence. (Compare the Padstow verse: 'I warn you young men every one....') The Minehead Horse is built on the same principle as the Padstow Oss, but on its canvas are painted many circles of various colours. The upper part and the conical cap are covered with hundreds of ribbons. The tail was not long ago a piece of rope (see quotation from Kille, p.13) though recently the cow's tail has been reintroduced. The mask is of tin. The accompanists are now confined to one drum and an accordion, though previously two men in fantastic costumes and masks known as Gullivers also accompanied the horse, carrying heavy clubs: compare the Padstow Teazer. These supporters would enter houses and demand money, but the practice was discontinued after a dispute between the Gullivers and a householder which ended fatally for the owner. The first act of the Minehead Horse and party is to visit the crossroads known as Whitecross, where formerly a May Pole used to be erected (compare Cross Street, Padstow, also the former site of a May Pole) and on May Day afternoon the Lord of the Manor at Dunster Castle is visited - as the Padstow Obby invariably visits Prideaux Place. Minehead's Horse is also apt to become mischievous, rushing at onlookers and swinging round to strike them with his tail. The Minehead folk claim that long ago a Padstow ship put into harbour, and the crew were so taken with the Hobby that they took it (whether Horse itself or only the idea is not clear) back to Padstow with them.

Helston Furry Day and Dance

As Claude Berry in his book on Cornwall remarked, certain similarities between Padstow's May Day and Helston Furry or Flora Day exist. Helston celebrates on May 8th, the original date of Beltane; now St. Michael's Day. It is not without significance that St. Michael the Archangel has replaced the Celtic sun-god Belinus in many places in Cornwall and also Brittany: St. Michael's Mount, the chapel of St. Michael on Roughtor, etc. So we may regard Helston Furry (Cornish Fer, a fair) as originally a Celtic summer welcoming, and not a Roman festival of the flower-goddess, Flora. Here again the Morris May-Games and Mummers' Plays have overlaid the original festivities, so that in the songs we find Robin Hood, Little John; St. George (and also St. Michael) as well as Aunt Mary Moyses, the Helston equivalent of Aunt Ursula Birdhood. (See Canow Kernow, p.12).

That the Padstow May Song and the Helston Hal-an-Tow are very close to each other in origin cannot be doubted. Both contain or contained the refrain 'In every land O, the land where 'er we go' and 'For to fetch home the summer and the May O, For summer is acome and winter is ago' - and also 'Hal-an-Tow! Jolly Rumble O!' The former Day Song at Padstow, as we have seen, began with "Awake St. George, our English Knight O...." The third verse of the Helston Hal-an-Tow goes:-

> As for that good knight St. George,
> St. George he was a knight, O!
> Of all the knights in Christendom
> St. George he is the right O.

Verse 2 of the Hal-an-Tow reads: 'Where are those Spaniards....'

Verse 2 of the Day Song reads: 'Where are the French dogs....'

One might expect the Helstonians to be more preoccupied with wars with Spain than with France.

Helston, like Padstow, goes to the greenwood to fetch the May home, not only in the song but actual performance. Inglis Gundry notes, of the name of Hal-an-Tow, that it may originate from the Dutch 'Haal aan het touw' (Heave on the rope) or English 'Haul and tow' - and quotes Nicholas Boson (1660) as recording that the May Pole at Newlyn was set up by men singing "Haile an Taw, and Jolly Rumbelow". But the phrase, which does not seem to be known outside Cornwall, may derive from the Cornish Halan (= 1st of the month), and Rumble O, which Gundry thinks means to move or stir actively, could derive from the Cornish Runen = horsehair. No doubt Helston, and Newlyn too, once had their Hobby Horses.

The development of Helston Furry Day has taken it in a different direction from Padstow. The Furry procession is led by the Mayor and civic dignity, and the dancers are dressed in traditional best - the men in morning coats and top hats, the ladies in long white dresses. But Padstow, as far as we know, has never had the honour of civic recognition. Spontaneity and democracy is all.

Connection between the Mummers Play and the May Day rites

Hall and Plunkett also suggest that the Padstow Obby Oss may originally have been a Christmas or New Year Mummers' Hobby Horse, which has strayed from its rightful place in the calendar, and become associated with the spring and fertility rites. They state that the life and death ritual proper is found almost exclusively in association with the Winter Solstice, and is the essence of the Folk Play, as performed in mid-winter. This is an interesting theory, especially in view of the reference to St. George in the Day Song, but one wonders whether these two ardent folklorists are not searching a little too hard for something which may not exist. Padstow did indeed have its own Mummers Play, performed for many years, unfortunately only now remembered and noted down in fragments: it concerned St. George and the Turkish Knight, who is duly killed and brought to life again. But it is impossible to say whether this play ever had a hobby horse (as many other Mummers Plays had). If indeed there is anything in this thesis, then not only Padstow, but the Minehead, the Coombe Martin, and the King's County hobby horse (which used to jump over fires on St. John's Eve) have all wandered from their correct dates. But the idea begs one question: if the Horse is the great symbol of fertility (see Harlow, p.12) why indeed should he have been associated with mid-winter, rather than any other season? All the evidence seems to point to the horse as being invoked at all and every seasons.

A May Day Ship?

Some writers have seen in the May Song a reference to a processional ship, formerly carried by the Mayers. M.A. Canney (Folklore, June 1938) asks 'did the May Day procession at Padstow include a ship, as appears in many other places?' He cites various other ship processions, all over Europe, including the Millbrook (Tamarside) May Day Ship which used to be carried through the streets, and the fact that until the late 18th to 19th century Padstow was a flourishing shipbuilding port. The verse referred to is:

> The young men of Padstow, they might if they would ......
>
> They might have built a ship and gilded her with gold ......

Certainly, gilding a ship would only have been done for ceremonial purposes. Perhaps here, too, another impressive part of the festivities has been lost to us during the changing centuries.

The Oss at Treator about 1897.
Dickie Brenton with drum. Chrissy-anna
and Ducker on right.

4. BACKALONG: 1800-1900

In attempting to trace, as far as the accounts of contemporary writers and artists can help us, the evolution and character of Padstow May festivities during the 19th century, we are faced with a fair amount of conflicting evidence. Some of it draws a picture of a custom falling into disrepute and drunkenness; other reports portray an idyllic annual event, almost too decorous to be believed. Certainly the Hobby Horse itself at the beginning of that century was a much smaller creature and occupied a less prominent place in the proceedings than it does now. The Rev. Richard Polwhele, whose History of Cornwall appeared in 1803, gives a bare picture suggesting a rather crude and earthy ceremony:

> On May 1st a festival is kept here (at Padstow) which is called the hobby horse, from a man being drest up in a stallion horse's skin, led by crowds of men and women thro' the streets, and at every dirty pool dipping the head in the pool and throwing out the water upon them. It is therefore the British festivity of May Day observed in a manner not British.

It is quite possible that Polwhele did not actually witness May Day at Padstow, but accepted hearsay reports of it. In 1817 C.S. Gilbert wrote in his Historical Survey of Cornwall:

> There is an annual jubilee kept up at Padstow on May 1st, known by the name of the Hobby Horse, in illusion to which the inhabitants dress up a man in a horse's skin, and lead him through the different streets. This odd-looking animal amuses, by many whimsical exploits, the crowd which follow at his heels, particularly by taking up dirty water wherever it is to be found, and throwing it into the mouths of his gaping companions. These tricks naturally produce shouts of laughter, and the merriments are accompanied by songs made for the occasion The origin of this festival appears to be unknown.

Hitchens and Drew (1824) were even more explicit about the rain-charm side of the proceedings:

> On the first of May, another species of festivity is pursued in Padstow. This is called The Hobby Horse; from canvas being extended with hoops, and painted to resemble a horse. Being carried through the streets, men, women and children, flock round it, when they proceed to a place called Traitor (sic) Pool, about a quarter of a mile distant, in which the hobby-horse is always supposed to drink; when the head being dipped into the water, is instantly taken up, and the mud and water are sprinkled on the spectators, to the no small diversion of all. On returning home, a particular song is sung, that is supposed to commemorate the event that gave the hobby-horse birth. According to tradition, the French on a former occasion effected a landing at a small cove in the vicinity; but seeing at a distance a number of women dress in red cloaks, which they mistook for soldiers, they fled to their ships, and put to sea. The day generally ends in riot and dissipation (Ex. Vol.I)
>
> Of the ancient custom of dressing up the hobby horse, the manner of conducting it to Treator-pool, and the sports accompanying its supposed drinking, an account has been given towards the conclusion of the preceding volume. Early in the morning which ushers in the first of May, the young people assemble, and sing through Padstow streets, a barbarous composition to rouse the inhabitants from their beds. What this composition originally was, it is impossible to say: but in its present state, it is too despicable for insertion. On marching to Treator-pool with the hobby horse, another dirge is set to music, which can hardly boast any superior excellencies to the former. From this strange but ancient composition, the two following verses are selected; which as they conclude the song, shall terminate the history of Padstow.
>
> > O where is St. George, O where is he O ?
> > He is in his long boat upon the salt sea O.
> > And for to fetch the summer home, the summer and the May O!
> > For summer is a come, and winter is ago.
> >
> > O where are the French dogs? they are on the coast O,
> > And they shall eat the grey goose feather, and we will eat the roast O!
> > And for to fetch the summer home, the summer and the May O,
> > For summer is a come, and winter is ago.
> >   (Ex Vol. II)

It is clear that in those days the original extended Day Song was sung on the way to Treator, which was looked upon as the home of the Oss. This reinforces the importance of the water-rite, and also possibly the theory of the Dragon and St. Petroc.

Apparently May 1st at Padstow was not a thing to be particularly proud of, in the eyes of these gentlemen. In 1830, according to West Briton reports, it was enlivened by a 'ram-riding', after the Oss had been stabled. Claude Berry describes this as 'not at all genteel': an event in which an erring pair of lovers - one of them an unfaithful husband or wife - were guyed, effigies of them being set up in a cart, which headed a procession of men and boys astride donkeys and blowing horns. In Berry's view, this affair was not related to the Ossing, but Miss Spooner has suggested that it may have been traditional to indulge in this sort of thing on May Day, and sees a reference to it in one of the verses of the former Day Song:

> Thou might'st have shown thy knavish face,
> Thou might'st have tarried at home O;
> But thou shalt be an old cuckold,
> And thou shalt wear the horns O.

The following year, 1831, the festivities concluded with the young people forming parties and going into the country 'to take tea, cream and syllabubs', and in the evening they joined in a dance. What, commented C.B., could be more innocent and pastoral? He also stated that apart from the ram-riding, he could find no adverse report on Padstow's May Day at this time.

Our next consecutive piece of evidence is the engraving, reproduced on p.11 which from the costumes depicted has been dated at 1840 (Violet Alford) and 1835 (Hall and Plunkett). This scene is also charming and innocent; the ladies in particular are well dressed, and certainly do not appear to be common folk; though it is just possible that they were fisherfolk dressed up, as we say, 'to the nines'. What is disconcerting is the next report, by Mr. George Rawlings, banker and Justice of the Peace, of Padstow, published in 1865 by Robert Hunt in his Popular Romances of the West of England:

> Formerly all the respectable people at Padstow kept this anniversary, decorated with the choicest flowers; but some unlucky day a number of rough characters from a distance joined in it, and committed some sad assaults upon old and young, spoiling all their nice summer clothes, and covering their faces and persons with smut. From that time - fifty years since - (1865) the procession is formed of the lowest.

Clearly there is a great discrepancy here. If Rawlings was right, May Day at Padstow became degraded about 1815; in this he is supported by Gilbert, Hitchens and Drew. But if the engraving and the West Briton of 1831 are to be believed, there must have been some return to respectability. Does all this matter? Probably not much: it all depended upon one's social standing and point of view. What was then degraded to the gentility (who were the purchasers of those weighty volumes on Cornwall) might well have been mere innocent amusement to the lower middle-class and working class people of Padstow

Before we leave the c. 1835 engraving, By T. or J. Lander of unknown history (certainly a Cornishman, one would expect, and therefore not an outsider whose picture might be suspect), certain aspects of it call for comment. The Oss is depicted without the mask we know today; but, as we shall see, this was a later addition after 1840. However the actual site is difficult to identify, especially as we know that in the mid-19th century the May Pole was always erected in Cross Street. (Mr. T.H. Williams believed it shows a green in front of the Manor House, before houses were built in St. Saviour's Lane, and that the hills in the background are the St. Minver Highlands: but if this was the artist's intention he has wrongly sited his May Pole, which appears to be down near the water). A man is climbing the May Pole, possibly an old custom now lost to us: during the 18th and 19th Centuries in Wales, according to Marie Trevelyan, the leader of the May dance would climb the Pole to affix a ribbon, and other dancers would then follow suit.

Whether the May Day Rites were actually respectable or not, one section of the community certainly disapproved of them and wished to end them: the non-conformist revivalists of the mid-19th century. About 1847 (the exact date has not been established), one Thomas Tregaskis, a merchant, farmer and local preacher, attempted to bribe the followers of the Oss to give up their 'vain practice' by offering a roasted bullock to be consumed in Padstow in place of the usual festivities. The Mayers rejected the proposal in the following terms, taken from a poster printed by them:

FELLOW TOWNSMEN

We have read the proposal Mr. Tregaskis made to the 'Proprietors of the Hobbyhorse', which we decidedly reject.

For several Years past, he, and his Family, have made ineffectual attempts to cry down the Hobby. In their system of annoyance they have resorted to the meanest stratagem to carry out their fanatical and visionary projects. We presume to offer a suggestion to the sagacious and liberal Sir Tommy, that will better develop and principle of sound philanthropy (sic), and a more effectual check to 'vain practices' than 'the Proprietors of the Hobbyhorse eating a Bullock for their rational amusement'. It is this, that at his next Teetotal Festival, instead of attracting a large assembly at S. Issey, to fill the Public House, and disgrace the occasion that called them together, he will issue a Proclamation to give every person gratuitously as much Cake and Tea (or a roasted Bullock if he would rather), as they choose to make use of. Charity would then begin at home, and inspire us with confidence in his principles, which we do not at present possess.

The bones of every Padstow Boy are fired by the Hobbyhorse. As soon as a child is able to lisp its parent's name it will chant the glorious strains of our ancient Festival Song; and will usher in May's first merry morn, with 'The summer, and the Summer, and the May, O!'

And shall we allow aliens and strangers to usurp our pleasures, and rob us of our birth-right, that we have inherited from Mother to Daughter, from Father to Son? No we will not: and poor Sir Tommy shall not be crowned King of the Hobbyhorse.

From the great encouragement we have received from every grade of society in town, we are determined the entertainments of this year shall greatly surpass precedings ones.

Given under the Great Seal of
'THE HOBBYHORSE FRATERNITY'

Thurstan Peter suggests that T. Tregaskis was born at Kea in 1785 and was a merchant of St. Issey. However, Claude Berry, whose access to the files of the West Briton from 1811 onwards makes him a more reliable commentator, says that Tregaskis was a well-known evangelist of the Carnon Valley district and that he drove his choice bullock all the way to Padstow.

Oss Masks

At some date after this the final and culminating development of the Oss itself took place, turning it into the ferocious monster - the true Cornish Oss we now know. Apart from size and colour, the main difference between Padstow's Obby Oss and other Hobbies is, of course, his mask. Padstow's is unique in the British Isles, being of immense savagery and of a design not seen anywhere else in Europe. Baring-Gould considered the red and white markings to be Celtic. He compared them with markings on various crosses and inscribed stones; Hall and Plunkett to Saxon and Jutish designs on 5th century graves. The Cadi, or Chief, of the Welsh May Games also at times wore a frightening mask daubed with red and white. But the similarity to certain tribal designs on shields and masks in West Africa, Malaysia and New Guinea is startling. Indeed, Douglas Neil Kennedy, President of the Folklore Society l (Encyclopaedia Mitannica Morris) writes:

Another comparable custom is that of the May Day procession of a man-horse, notably at Padstow in Cornwall. There the central figure "Oss Oss" (sic) is a witch doctor disguised as a horse and wearing a medicine mask.

Mr. T.H. Williams reasoned that at some date a Padstow man probably brought the original mask back from some voyage to the East or Africa; and further guessed that the O.B. marking on the cap was the initials of the sailor who introduced it. The Brenton family seemed the most likely supposition. He supported his view with the fact that many of the Ossing party were men who signed on ships, some of which sailed from Padstow itself during its great days as a trading and ship-building port, and sailed round the world. No other satisfactory explanation of the O.B. marking has been arrived at: though Dr. Tabb, Bard Map Lodenek, suggested that they commemorate Obba, a Danish chief said to be active in this area during the 10th Century.

Mr. Williams is almost certainly correct in his deductions. There is a tradition in the Brenton family that Octavious, uncle of Harry Brenton (Signior Brintano, Oss Poster 1912 - see p.22) first brought the mask to Padstow from one of his voyages; to be adopted, against what acclaim or disapproval can only be surmised, by the Ossers. Harry Brenton himself always maintained that the mask 'didn't really belong'. But nowadays, a hundred years or so since its introduction, it is established as a permanent feature of May Day, which would now be as unthinkable without it as without the May Song itself.

The date was evidently some years before 1865, since we know from George Rawlings' account that the mask was being worn then:

> The horse is formed as follows: The dress is made of sackcloth painted black - a fierce mask - eyes red, horse's head, horse-hair mane and tail; distended by a hoop - some would call it frightful. Carried by a powerful man, he could inflict much mischief with the snappers, etc. No doubt it is a remnant of the ancient plays, and it represents the devil, or the power of darkness. They commence singing at sunrise.

Hall and Plunkett (Ethnic, Summer 1959) give an interesting series of drawings comparing masks and snapper designs of various Osses through the years.

'Pairs'

The term 'pair' first occurs in Bewnans Meriasek (see p.10): 'I will pay out the Hobby Horse and its pair.'

Baring Gould, writing in 1889, described (p.19) the Ossing party of the day as The Hobby Horse Pairs, i.e., a party of eight men. Mr. T.H. Williams believed that Lander's engraving purported to show four pairs of dancers, gentlemen and ladies, though one lady is missing. Thurstan Peter, in 1913, also refers to 'The Hobby Horse Pairs', though he does not number them. In the photo of the Old Oss taken at Treator (pre 1900) it is difficult to decide who is a member of the party and who are spectators, but certainly the party could not have exceeded eight in number. Hall and Plunkett state that in 1889 when William (Bluey) England first joined the Oss party, there were eight of them - six men and two women. See also the photos of the Oss, on p.11 and p.15. It is only since 1919 that the Oss party has grown to the size it is now, and the term 'pairs' is no longer used.

The May Pole

Henry Harding, printer of Padstow (see broadsheet reproduced on back cover) wrote (in 1883) in the Western Antiquary: 'The May Pole on the 1st of May at Padstow has only been discontinued within the last six or eight years'. He was referring to the traditional May Pole at Cross Street, of which Baring Gould had this to say:

> During the evening before May Day in years past, before ship-building had ceased to be an industry of Padstow, when the shipwrights left work, they brought with them from the yard two poles, and carried them up the street, fastened one above the other, decorated the top with branches of willow, furze, sycamore, and all kinds of spring flowers, made into garlands, and from it suspended strings of gulls' eggs, which the young men had been out on the cliffs and islets collecting. There hung from it also long streamers of coloured ribbon.
> A pit was dug, and the May Pole secured by ropes fastened to stakes. It stood, within the memory of man, at a crossing of streets where there was a tolerably open space. In the pavement was a cross laid in with different coloured paving stones to the rest of the street, and these stones were taken up every time the Maypole was planted, to be again replaced when the merrymaking was over. But a doctor who lived in the house facing the pole objected, and so opposed the planting of the pole and the dancing before his door that the merrymakers moved to a less convenient spot higher up the street. Opposition followed them, and a few years ago the May Pole was finally abandoned.
> The fixing the May Pole and dressing it was of great interest to all; not even the children could be got to go to bed till it was finished.

Thurstan Peter notes that the May Pole was often as much as 90ft. high - which may seem difficult to believe, for it must have rivalled the church tower! However we should remember that Padstow was at that time building tall-masted sailing ships, and the maypole was traditionall supplied by one of the shipyards. The May Pole being discontinued, Padstow was without one apart from an odd year or two, until after the first world war, when (see p.9) the site chosen was Broad Street; where it has been erected every year since. Decorations have varied; no gulls eggs have been used, but much fastidious work has gone into these erections with results that have certainly enhanced May Day. In this connection the artistry of Mr. W.H. Chapman, whose Sun-Food Stores dominated Broad Street, was for a number of years a pleasure to behold.

The siting of the original May Pole at Cross Street was not accidental. The Minehead Hobby Horse traditionally goes to crossroads at Whitecross, where a May Pole was erected for centuries previously. Thurstan Peter saw this as significant, and quotes John O'Neil's "The Night of the Gods" to show that in pre-Christian times sacrifices to various gods were made at crossroads. Many May Poles elsewhere have specially made dolls suspended from them, which are seen by some authorities to be replacements of children offered for spring sacrifice.

Maypoles, of course, were formerly to be seen everywhere in Britain on May 1st. Parliament banned them in 1644, but the Restoration of Charles II saw one 134 feet high erected in the Strand, London. Many poets, from Spenser to Pope, have mentioned Maypoles.

Pistols

The tradition of firing off blank-loaded pistols on May Day is a very interesting, if perplexing one. The earliest evidence of it is our engraving of c.1835. As Mr. T.H. Williams observed, the pistols are apparently being fired from the four points of the compass, which may be a piece of Christian symbolism or a pagan one stemming from crossroads folklore. Baring Gould wrote of May Day at Padstow, (1889): 'Formerly as many as two hundred men carried pistols in the procession'. Thurstan Peter wondered whether the pistols represented the wars against the French, mentioned in the May Song, or were purely intended to increase the noise and general celebration. He writes that pistols were said to have been discontinued after the new police were introduced (after 1840). It is tempting to see a relationship between pistol firing and the Beltane fires, and a popular tradition in Padstow has been that the guns were fired in dark corners to banish winter. However it should be borne in mind that all over Cornwall pistol firing as part of any celebration (e.g. weddings) was popular during the late 18th and early 19th centuries.

Night Singing

This is the term used to distinguish this custom from the day-proceedings. The song sung, of course, is the Morning Song, which has now become attenuated to four verses on the Blue Ribbon Oss sheet. But many of the other verses now printed as the Day Song are used, so perpetuating the pre-1914 usage.

Baring Gould's 1889 account of this part of May Day is as follows:

> The "Hobby-horse Pairs" as it was called, i.e. a party of eight men, then repaired to the Golden Lion, at that time the first inn in Padstow, and sat down to a hearty supper given them by the landlord. After supper a great many young men joined the "Pairs" - the peers, Lords of Merriment - and all started for the country to visit the farmhouses and solicit contributions towards the festivities of the morrow.

He does not mention that Prideaux Place is visited. Thurstan Peter quotes J. Walker Tyacke, a Padstonian, who wrote in 1912:

> After supper they make a round of the countryside and town, singing in front of the more important houses (including the Vicarage, which they formerly reached at midnight.

The Vicarage was then the Old Vicarage, on the Newquay Road opposite the cemetery. It seems clear from these accounts that the night singing began long before midnight; according to Thurstan Peter it went on in 1913 until 2.0 a.m., to the annoyance of some residents.

Red Oss - Blue Oss

These are the popular terms which have crept in to represent the Old Oss and the Blue Ribbon Oss. Have there always been two Osses? Almost certainly not; C.S. Gilbert, G. Rawlings, Baring Gould, all mention only one. We know that in the 1880's William (Bluey) England made several Osses and ran a rival party; Thurstan Peter (1913) commented:

> More recently (than Tregaskis' attempt to ban the Oss) the unco guid introduced a rival horse, white, with accompanying anaemic ceremony. It is to be hoped none will mistake the two horses as winter and summer!

Mr. Peter appears to have been somewhat misled by his informant, doubtless a loyal Old Oss man. 'Bluey' did, for May Day one year (which? - no photo seems to have survived) produce a white Oss, but discontinued it in face of general disapproval. His other Osses were known as Blue Ribbon Osses, and there is a definite connection here with the Temperance Movement, organised sections of which paraded in Blue Sashes at anniversaries. Peter's reference to 'the unco quid' supports this. However 'Bluey' became a great Ossing character and it is an unjust criticism to dub his ceremony as anaemic. It may have been a little more decorous than the boisterous Old Oss, but those who can remember the two parties describe it as traditional in form and dance. In 1912 (see p. 23) there were <u>three</u> main Osses! The third was almost certainly the one mentioned by the Guardian in 1913 as being kept at the Lower Shipyard.

It is worth noting here that in 1881 Padstow Institute was built, on the site of the old London inn, with publicly raised funds to provide a place of 'mental and moral relaxation for the men of Padstow', where they would not be confronted by the evils of drink. In those days drink was certainly an evil, being cheap and plentiful, and the port of Padstow had little to offer men in the way of entertainment apart from its numerous inns. So William England's attempt to create a more respectable Oss no doubt had the encouragement of the Wesleyan, Bryanite and temperance sections of the community; although according to Mr. W.H. Thomas of Duke Street, Padstow, it did not collect for charity, but, like the Old Oss, for the personal profit of its party.

Teazers' Masks, similar to the mask of the Oss itself, have at various times in the past been worn. Thurstan Peter records one being worn in 1913, and we have a photo of that approximate time (see p. 5) to prove it. The Blue Ribbon Teazer's mask, worn after World War II, was modelled and made by Mr. David Farquhar (Senior); it replaced a previous mask, which had been a conical Teazer's hat of the same shape as the Oss mask with a pigtail of horsehair hanging down behind.

The 1913 teazer danced in a long-nose mask. Today Teazer's masks are not used, being said to be too hot and uncomfortable; but it should now be possible to construct one of lighter man-made material. Without these masks something of Padstow's originality is lost.

Teazers' Clubs

The clubs have considerably varied in design and construction over the years. Some designs are shown on p 26

Hall and Plunkett show ten of them. The usual form is of a black leather padded top on a wooden handle; lambswool has been the usual padding, and forms the trimming as well, though ribbons sometimes serve. The club is related to the Morris fool's bladder on a stick, said to represent the uterus; Padstow clubs can generally however be considered phallic in form. Although nowadays the Dancer often lays, even drags his club on the ground, this was previously (pre-1914) never done. In c 1919 photo the club appears to be hinged, but it may possibly have broken during the days' activities.

Flowers

The Garlanding of the May Pole, and the bringing home of the May, have already been referred to. Miss Courtney (1890) stated that 'the week before Flora-day is in Helston devoted to the "spring-clean" and every house is made "as bright as a new pin" and the gardens stripped of their flowers to adorn them'; Thurstan Peter adds in a footnote that Padstow folk considered they had a right to strip anyone's garden, and the police at times had to interfere. He noted that the 'pairs' of her day wore wreaths of sycamore with bluebells, tulips, cowslips, etc., and the men often carried a tulip in their mouths. This differs from the general Morris tradition which is to dress in ribbons and bells, and would appear to be a direct association with the fertile powers of nature.

The May Lady and Female Impersonation

The tradition of having a female character to accompany the Oss is one which goes back to the days of the introduction of the Morris. The May Lady represented Maid Marian, known in later (Tudor and Stuart) times as Malkin, and was usually played by a man in a woman's costume. Our Oss has adopted Aunt Ursula as his 'mistress', it seems: Thurstan Peter says that Mr. Docton and Mr. M.A.C. Trebilcock (both previously referred to) maintained that in the middle of the 19th century one of the Mayers was always an old woman in a scarlet cloak and cape. From 1889 to about 1914 there were two women Mayers, Chrissie Anna Bray and Elizabeth 'Ducker' Prynne. (see Treator photo, p.15). About this time 'Dolly' (Captain H. Dennant) was dressing up as a woman and taking part in the proceedings. After 1920 Mr. W.H. Thomas continued this tradition (see p.26) which he maintained until the mid-1960's. Meanwhile J.H. MacOwen - 'Lively Mac', as he was known until his later years, the Old Oss' leading Teazer, - often dressed as a woman during the 'thirties.

Luck and Fertility

Another tradition associated with Ossing is that a woman who is 'caught' by the Oss - i.e. trapped in under its skirts - will become 'lucky' or pregnant. Thurstan Peter says, 'luck no longer defined but understood to encourage child-bearing'. Mr. W.H. Thomas recalls seeing unmarried women running the length of whole streets to escape rather than be caught, for this reason. More recently women, as if in time with more modern attitudes, have taken part in the capture as a matter of sport and enjoyment. It would seem that the abduction of married women, especially those who were childless, was sought after in pre-Victorian times, thus supporting the theory of the Oss representing a Corn or Fertility Spirit. Thurstan Peter also quotes Beatrice F. Cresswell and others as saying at that time (1911-12) 'sometimes married women will court the hobby's touch and single women avoid it'. In Julius Caesar is a reference to horse-touching bringing fertility: the childless Calpurnia is told by Caesar to stand in the way of Antony's horse as he rides in the 'holy race' - a celebration for victory - presumably so that she will no longer be barren.

"Wee Oss" - and the chase

Many strangers to the town are mystified by the Mayers' cry 'Oss-Oss!' and the thunderous response from Padstonians of 'Wee Oss!' This 'war cry' seems to be a relic of Morris rather than of Padstow itself. Baring Gould quotes the dramatist John Fletcher (1579-1625) who in his play 'Women Pleased' wrote this speech for a Puritan character:

    This beast of Babylon (the Hobby-horse) I'll ne'er back again,
    His pace is sure prophane, and his lewd Wi-hees!
    . . . . . .
    I do defy thee and thy footcloth too. . .
    This unedified ambling hath brought a scourge upon us.

The similarity between 'Wi-hees' and Wee Oss suggests that these are in fact two versions of the same cry. Violet Alford (Folklore, 1939) interpreted it as meaning 'Come to us, Oss'. Baring Gould (1889) reports 'Wee Oss! Follow my Hoss!' uttered in a peculiar tone. Miss Spooner held 'Wee Oss' to be an equine imitatory whinny to encourage the Oss, & quoted an old Padstow woman as saying, 'He's pretty wheeing'. But, comparing Fletcher's speech with Padstow practice, it seems certain that it was originally a cry to encourage the Oss to capture and mate symbolically with the woman he was pursuing. Thurstan Peter says that 'O Wee Oss' was shouted in 1913 by everyone when the Oss pursued some 'victim'. Miss Alford in 1968 recorded that Swiss carnival hobbies recited poems and ended them with 'Whee-hee' and declares that traditionally, and as recorded by 'our Elizabethan dramatists' this should be answered by the female 'Ti-Hee'. The derivation of 'Wee Oss' therefore appears to be from the horse-whinny.

The Peace Oss and team 1919
Market (Island site)

Visit of the Peace Oss to the
Royal Albert Hall, 1927.

5. THE TWENTIETH CENTURY

By the early 1900's the way Padstow celebrated May Day was not, on the whole, held in great approval by its better-class inhabitants: as witness the account entitled 'Padstow Saturnalia', written by Mr. Sandford Allport, insurance and customs agent and general pillar of the community (quoted in 'Days in Cornwall' by Lewis Hind). Allport considered it 'ludicrous', 'a very rough and coarse pastime', and 'a relic of barbarism'; the latter comment being fair enough no doubt, but not in the sense in which it was then intended. The custom had survived in that gentleman's opinion because 'the principal actors get a little money out of it, and the youngsters, who follow, an abundance of fun and frolic'. The May Song, he said, was 'doggerel without rhyme or reason', and concluded, 'the whole affair is gradually dying out, to the honour of the town, and ere long may be consigned to the limbo of the past'.

He was wrong, of course. A few years later Cecil Sharp visited Padstow, took photos of the Oss and noted down the May Song, and the folk revival embraced Padstow. Allport's account was certainly an oversimplification. The character of May Day at Padstow during this period (1901-1918) may be better gauged by the following accounts of proceedings, taken from Padstow news items in the Cornish Guardian:

1901 'Today the discordant sounds which proclaim the presence of the Hobby Horse greet our ears, and the May Song is rapturously sung by persons of every age. In all parts of the world where Padstonians reside they think of home today and talk to each other about the old custom which they still so pleasantly remember: for notwithstanding its somewhat repellant character it is still regarded with some sort of affection by all who in their childhood took such an interest in it.'

1902 was a quiet May Day. The Guardian congratulated everyone on the 'lack of disorder'.

1903 was not a good year. The Guardian, appearing on the May Day itself, hoped for great things:-
'May Day this year is likely to be exceptionally interesting. The town is alive with joyful anticipation. Efforts are being made to array the dancers in gay costumes for the occasion. We thought the custom would have been swept away by the flowing tide of criticism, but it seems as vigorous as ever - more now than for a considerable period, some people would say!'

But a week later, on May 8th, it recorded a sad tale:
'The May Day celebrations of which we wrote an account last week, were a disappointment in consequence of the unusual amount of drunkenness that met our eyes. Not for many years have we witnessed such sights as greeted us last Friday. Much as we respect old customs and tolerate slight deviations from every day life, we are quite of the opinion that it would be better for the Hobby Horse to become a thing of the past than for it to continue and be accompanied by such disgraceful manifestations: in fact conduct of that order will of itself kill the old custom which Padstonians have so long enjoyed.'

1904 was unremarkable, except for certain incidents the Guardian did not record. In 1905 it said, 'May Day was a usual characterised by the old weird custom of the Hobby Horse, in which only natives of Padstow can see much to be desired. We are glad however that it was accompanied this year with considerably less drunkenness, and we hope that the disturbances were not such as to lead to magisterial enquiries as was the case last year.'

By 1908 May Day was though to be again on the downpath: 'The singing is declining yearly and general interest is diminishing. After visiting Treator the 'Hoss' returned and made a full tour of the main streets until the Golden Lion was reached and he was put in his stable for another year.

In 1909 'May Day was kept up in the usual fashion. The 'hosses' and some colts paraded the town and district. To the uninitiated the whole process is too ridiculous for words but to the native who knows the historical meanings of the proceedings it is an anniversary to be proud of.'
In the evening the local Territorials held a May Day shoot, a regular event with them.

In 1910 no better opinion of the proceedings was held by the newspaper, but the festivities themselves were evidently livelier: 'No sign of any abatement of what many consider to be a nuisance. The town was gaily decorated and the old Hoss, rejuvenated, caused much merriment and pleasure of a sort. The fishermen here recently caught an unknown fish of remarkable appearance, but they admit they have never netted such a hideous monster as our "Hoss".'

By 1911 due to the fondness of Lowestoft trawlermen for the event (during this year 400 trawlers put into Padstow), May Day was beginning to be truly popular: 'The Hobby Horses on coming out at 10.30 were immediately joined by crowds of people composed mainly of fisherfolk who seem to take a great interest in this old custom. About half a dozen of them dressed themselves in ladies' fashionable attire, one even wearing the harem skirt which caused great amusement, and every one seemed to join in heartily in the fun, which was kept up to a late hour.'

In 1912 the staid and august Guardian reprinted details of the poster put out by the combined Oss parties:

> Programme of the Ossy League, May 1, 1912, under direction of the Marquis of Cove, K.C.S.
>
> 4.0 a.m. Duet 'The Ossy Morn is Dawning' by the Hotel & Rock View Cock, specially trained by Prof. Samuel Tildes.

6.0 a.m.	Peal on bells, 'Ossy Echoes'.
8.0 a.m.	Meet of the Ossy League at the Golden Lion.
10.15 a.m.	Preliminary Roll by Signior Brintano.
10.30 a.m.	Start, carried by Don Carlo de Bato.
10.45 a.m.	Snapper Dance by Lively Mac.
12.00 a.m.	Treator. May Song by Massed Ossy Choirs.
12.30 p.m.	Oss fed by the Countess of Mantlebury.
2.30 p.m.	Market Square. Juggling Display 'The Magnetic Broom' by Prof. Coo.
3.00 p.m.	Dance by Oss Damsels, introducing Skirt Dances by various artists.
3.30 p.m.	May Ring Dance by combined Osses.
	Snapper Duet by Bato & Vanguard.
4.00 p.m.	Entertainment by Fish Buyers, Salesmen, Packers and Skippers, introducing Dolly & Scarlo in their famous Lowestoft Twist.
8.00 p.m.	Cinematography, 'Nibble & Nance' in 'Adrift on the King's Highway'.

The report stated, 'Inclement weather did not prevent the attendance of a large number of followers of the <u>three Hobby Horses</u> parading the principal streets. Very few trawlers were in the harbour so amusement caused by fisherfolk on these crafts was missed.' (Editor's underlining – D.R.R.)

1913 was a disappointing year. 'The big Oss appeared before dinnertime, but the usual fun was lacking. Some of the young men borrowed another Oss from the Lower Yard. This soon attracted a large following and this was the best part of the day's proceedings.'

1914 was a good year. For the first time, large number of visitors were reported watching the festivities.

1915: The Oss is recorded as appearing at 11.0 a.m. and dancing until 7.30 p.m. Perhaps owing to the war fewer people were in evidence.

In 1916 the Guardian commented that never had the May Song been sung in so many parts of the globe before, as on this May morning with Padstow men away in the forces. The 'nocturnal heralding' of summer was rather weak owing to the lack of young men.

The war ended in 1918 and a new era began the following May Day.

The 'Peace Oss'

In 1919 a group of young Padstow men, returning from war service, built the 'Peace Oss', a slightly larger version than the Old Oss, which still continued. (See photo, p. 21, taken in the yard of the Market, or 'Island' site, which became the Peace or Blue Ribbon Oss's home for over 40 years). Set up with a Committee to revitalise May Day, and with the avowed intention of collecting for charitable causes, the **Peace Team** (who distinguished their Oss with a beard and a red, white and blue ribbon around its hoop), soon attracted considerable support. Five of the team performed with their Oss at the English Folk Dance & Song Society's display at the Royal Albert Hall in 1927: a major development which led to the Padstow May Day becoming much more popular and prized among those genuinely interested in British folk-lore and customs. Other visits, by both Osses, have followed with great success.) In other ways also the Peace Oss Committee made much more of May Day than hitherto. The Cornish Guardian recorded:

This year (1919) the chief feature was the advent of a new 'Peace' Hoss accompanied by a band of young men collecting for St. Dunstan's Hostel for blinded soldiers and sailors. Much amusement was caused by the apparent fright of many visitors at the strange apparition of the "Hoss".'

The May Pole was erected in Broad Street, the first in Padstow for some years. May Day itself, apart from the Ossing, was considerably expanded and enlivened.

In the evening, the Padstow Boys Fife & Drum band parade, played selections including May Song and Flora Dance, which was danced through the streets. 'Padstonians were extremely pleased with the whole day. Of late years the ancient custom of the Hobby Horse has been on the decline, but with the return of the younger men from the war a new effort was made this year and has been crowned with success. It is hoped that the Hobby Horse will regain the prestige it held in old days. Collectors received £20 above expenses, and this is being sent to St. Dunstan's.'

In 1920 'On Friday at midnight the combined Ossy choirs rendered the Morning Song in various parts of the town. At 10.0 a.m. the original Hobby Horse, whose headquarters is the Golden Lion, made its appearance accompanied by the usual retinue. The ancient Brenton drum was very much in evidence. About 1.0 p.m. the Comrade's Victory Horse came out and paraded the town collecting for their band instruments fund.' (Evidently a third Oss.) At 6.30 p.m. there was a Flora Dance, led by band, but it rained. Some £9.3.0. was collected. 'A number of visitors watched the proceedings with interest.'

1921: The Comrades Band again played in the evening and the people danced to it round the May Pole in Broad Street.

Until now the Guardian had reported May Day as a paragraph among others under the Padstow News Items. In 1922 a young reported named Claude Berry wrote the first full report in its own right, extending it to three columns of half a page in length. He began by quoting a popular jingle:

> 'O Where are you going to my pretty maid?
> I'm going a-Maying, sir, she said.
> What of your counter and customers, pray?
> O let them go hang - this is Hobby-Horse Day!'

Claude quoted the whole May Song, as per the 1903 broadsheet, 'since', he wrote, 'most of it has hushed into forgetfulness.'

1922 was said to be the most spirited and successful May Day for many years. The names of the carriers of two Osses in the evening around the May Pole were given: Frank and William Bray (Peace Oss) and Walter Bate (Old Oss). This year the British Legion Band led the evening Flora round the town. Afterwards a Mr. Harry Leslie tried to give a 'complete rendering' of the song at the Public room, but audience joined in and spoiled it. 'We didn't get the complete song after all'. Claude finished his account by making a plea for practice of whole song beforehand: a plea that has been repeated by many, year after year ever since, and one that is yet to be satisfactorily answered.

The Oss, in fact, was regaining respectability. Over the years the 'Peace Oss' and Blue Ribbon collections have realised many hundreds of pounds for the old people of Padstow; they have collected for Bodmin and Truro hospitals, for the St. Ives Lifeboat disaster of 1939, and as above for St. Dunstan's Hospital, among other causes. At one time between 1939-45 three Lowestoft sailors, lodging at the Seamen's Mission in Station Road, were given money to send home to their wives.

Among the original Peace Ossers in the photo are Percy Stribley, Archie Gard and W.H. (Bill) Thomas in the mask, a relic of Darky Days. Later Mr. E.P. (Percy) Stribley recorded the following notes on the 1919 Peace Oss, which had by then (after the 2nd World War) adopted the name of Blue Ribbon Oss.

Hoop recovered from Cowl's shipbuilding yard. Also snappers. Cap made by Thomas Peter Courtney. Gown material, the boys paid for, also the ribbon.
Gown was made by Miss Dorothy Stribley. Painting and decorations to cap and snappers by Gill England. Paint given by Frank Harvey. All collections to St. Dunstans. £26. No deductions.
Some names connected to the starting of the Peace Oss: Arch Gard, Perce Stribley, Harvey Mitchell, Frank Bray, Alec Hornabrook, Will Brabyn, Joe Apps, Harry Tucker, W.H. Thomas, Will Sleeman and many others.
Both the Night and Day Songs in the opinion of everyone was the best ever heard in Padstow; and no wonder, for some of Padstow best singers were doing their best.
Today by some Big mistake the Peace Oss is known as the Blue Ribbon Oss. True, there was a Blue Ribbon Oss and Will England (Bluey) was the chief, with Jim Stone, Jumbo MacOwen, Charlie Bate and others. But the Blue Ribbon was pre-1914, and as stated Temperance was the theme. But the Peace Oss was in no way connected with the Blue Ribbon Oss.

Blue Ribbon Osses have tended to be larger than the Old Oss. One, made just after the 2nd war, was the largest, measuring over 6ft. in diameter, but was found to be too big for efficiency.

CONSTRUCTION

The form of the Padstow Oss has developed as we have seen from the traditional Morris Hobby, with a mere three-feet diameter hoop (see Lander's engraving) to the impressive monster he is today. Although the earliest reports (Polwhele and Gilbert) mention horse-hide as being used for the gown, since 1824 (Hitchens and Drew) the recognised material has been canvas - tarred or lampblacked up till about 1890, and since then painted black.

The recently discarded Old Oss hoop was of teak and is around 120 years old; it is studded with nails of all ages. The oak snappers on which the date 1802 was found (see Thurstan Peter's account) were broken in 1969 and are now in the custody of Mr. Ernest Bate. The present Old Oss has an elm hoop, 5'9" in diameter and 18 feet in circumference. Its gown is of heavy sailcloth with skirts 4 feet in depth. (Until the 1920's skirts were much longer - practically down to the ground when carried.) Webbing shoulder braces, introduced, it is said, by Bluey England around the turn of the century, are now invariably used: without them, splitting of the canvas around the neck and warping of the hoop were disadvantages which can be seen in several photos of the period.

The whiskers on the mask are of natural sheep's wool, which is also used to pack the Teazer's club. Horse-hair is used on the conical hat, the tail and the mane of the snappers. The 'teeth' of the snappers are hob-nails, and the tongue is of leather painted red.

The Blue Ribbon Osses have followed the Old Oss in all details of construction, except that a wool beard is added to the mask. The hoop of the Peace Oss of 1919 was said to have been made from three lifeboat drogue hoops. For two years now however the Blue Ribbon gown has been of black terylene sailcloth, considerably lightening the burden.

Musical Accompaniments

These have varied considerably over the years. Thurstan Peter says that some fifty or sixty years previously (to 1913) the side drum and fife were prominent instruments, and Baring-Gould (1889) mentions only a drum and fife band. The second musician in the 1835 engraving plays a fife. Melodeons and later accordions came into use, and being the most suitable accompaniment for loudness, vigour and transportability, have since been the recognised May Day instrument. But a photo of the 1910 Oss team shows accompanists with banjo and tambourine - no doubt also used in connection with 'Darky' (Nigger Minstrel) activities on Boxing Day and New Years Day in Padstow. A photo of the same time shows Col. Bate with a triangle. In 1914 a valve trombone and cymbals were to be seen, and in 1937 a ukele appeared. An Anglo-German concertina was played pre-1914. But the great basis of all May Day music is the drum, which seems to take us back to the earliest times with its powerful rhythms. Padstow's May Day without drums would be impossible. The most famous drum of all is the Brenton, or Waterloo Drum, said to have been brought back by one of that family from the French Wars in 1815, which still booms out more effectively than any other. This may well be the deep drum depicted in Lander's 1835 engraving.

Today the size of the orchestras, like the Oss himself, has grown. The Blue team boast some six melodeons, two or three piano or push-button accordions, and three tenor drums. The Red or Old Oss team usually has five accordions and three drums, plus the Brenton.

Boys' Osses

Present-day 'Colts' or boys' Osses are the inheritors of a long tradition. Baring-Gould mentions them, accompanying their songs with triangles and tin whistles. Thurstan Peter says "In 1913 there were some smaller, badly shaped hobbies known as 'colts', the result apparently of the degeneration of the ritual into a mere excuse for collecting money." He would, one hopes, be more impressed by the boys' Osses of later years, some of which have been fine specimens, and have drawn the crowds' attention by their dancing. At present the local Cub troop mans a well-constructed Oss: which appeared at Piran Round 1970 as part of a performance of the play 'Petroc of Cornwall'. Baring-Gould notes that the boys always finished before the 'real Hobby' came out. The same was still true in 1914, though today they tend to stay and try to compete!

Mr. Walter 'Colonel' Bate recalls as a youth in his teens dancing in the White Oss, mentioned by Thurstan Peter, which was kept in the same stable as the Old Oss at the Golden Lion, between 1900 and 1903. With his brother John, and Jim Dale, he took it out in the morning before the Old Oss's appearance. This creation of Bluey's, a little smaller than the senior Oss, was at that time the main youth performer. Mr. W.H. Thomas recalls going out with a boys' team before 1914 to visit Treator, Windmill, Trevone and Porthmissen.

For Coronation year, 1937, some of the townswomen, including that well-remembered and loved character Rosie Walker, (Sorensen), had their own Oss: a dangerous precedent by some standards (see p. 12 Harlow), but one should also remember Aunt Ursula and her 'women's team'!

The Farewell Song is a much later addition to the proceedings. Both Oss parties sing it as a finale, but it was introduced by one of the Peace team, Mr. W.H. Thomas, about 1920. The words, which are from a Victorian ballad, are:

> One parting kiss I give thee,
> May nevermore behold thee – (alternatively: I cannot bear to leave thee)
> I go where duty calls me –
> I go whate'er befalls me:
> Farewell, farewell, my own true love.
> Farewell, farewell, my own true love.

This may be criticised from one point of view as an unnecessary innovation, but, like the singing of 'Tom Bowling' in the local Mummers' Play, is now such an integral part of the proceedings that it may be regarded as a folk song in the making.

Some Ossing Personalities – past and present

William Henry Baker: 1856 – 1924
    'Marquis of Cove' (Oss poster, 1912). Was Cox'n of lifeboat Arab; a man of immense strength who would carry the old Oss all day on occasions. Famous, or notorious, as a pursuer of women – in his Ossing capacity. Is said to have climbed a ship's rigging in his Oss, jumped the churchyard wall, etc.

Capt. Henry ('Dolly') Dennant: 1867 – 1934.
    A Lowestoft trawler skipper who took a prominent part, especially in pre-1914 May Days. Dressed as a woman, around 1910-12 in hobble and harem skirts. 'Dolly' on Oss poster, 1912.

William 'Bluey' England: 1870 – 1962.
    First accompanied the Oss in 1889. Before 1914 made several himself, known as Blue Ribbon (Temperance) Osses. His only absence in seventy years of Maying was during the siege of Ladysmith. Grand Old Man of Peace/Blue Ribbon Team until his death.

John Henry (Mac) MacOwen: 1871 – 1956.
    Known as 'Lively Mac' pre-1914 and during '20s: 'Old Mac' after 1945. A great leader and teazer. Dressed as it pleased him: in kilt, 1924; as a woman during the thirties; as harlequin, 1935-8.

William Vivian: 'Trevethan Red'.
    A celebrated character of inter-war years; came down each year from St. Mabyn, his home, and imbibed so well during May Day and successive days that he usually spent the following fortnight in Padstow, sleeping on the stairs at the back of the Golden Lion.

Head of "the 'oss"

c. 1889

The Yard of the Golden Lion from which the procession starts

c. 1889

TEAZER'S CLUBS

1928 Blue

1959 Red

1914

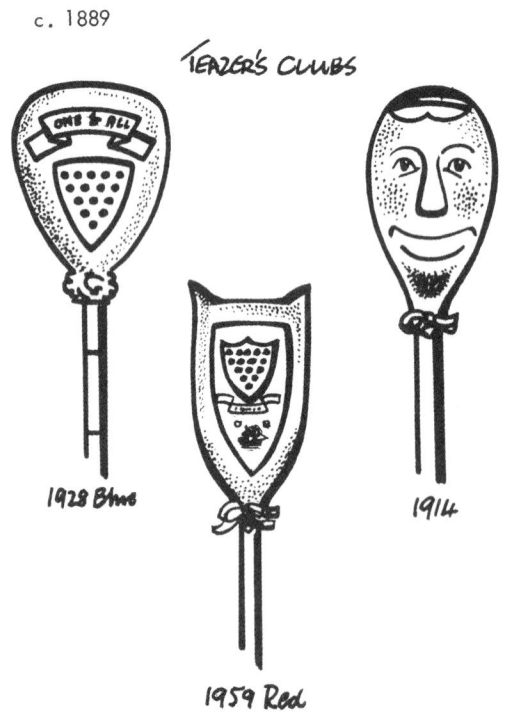

Peace Oss with May Lady (W.H. Thomas) and Teazer's Mask late 1940's.

26

Chrissana Bray and Elizabeth 'Ducker' Edwards (Prynne):
: Two steadfast women mayers, two of the number who made up the Pairs of the 1880's, '90's and early 1900's. Turned out in Sunday best with white pinafores. Elizabeth kept ducks — and plucked them.

Fred 'Jumbo' MacOwen: 1880 – 1926.
: One of the most artistic teazers ever to dance before the Oss: the pre-1914 Blue Ribbon and post-war Peace Oss.

Thomas Charles 'Wot Wether' Gregor: 1893 – 1955.
: Always cheery and ready with a quip or memorable phrase. Master of Ceremonies, Old Oss team, for some 20 years.

Walter ('Colonel') Bate: 1886 – 1973.
: Until his 87th year, the G.O.M. of the Old Ossers. Took part for 66 years; first carried the Oss in 1904, aged 18, and made a name for himself as one of the most vigorous dancers. Served 50 years with Padstow lifeboat crew. Led Old Oss party at Royal Albert Hall, during the Festival of Britain, 1951. Recalled going out to Treator until 1925.

Roderick Roseveare: 1912 – 1965
: A man of great stature, affectionately remembered by all. Was Old Oss M/C until his sudden death.

William Henry ('Bill') Thomas: 1894 – 1977.
: M/C Blue Ribbon Team during late 1960's and '70's. Main Teazer from 1920's, and famous in dress and make-up as May Lady for forty years. One of the five Ossers who took the Peace Oss to the Albert Hall, 1927.

Sammy Fielding:
: A Padstonian who always made for home just before May Day. Once walked home from Liverpool. Sometimes overcome by the proceedings and followed the Oss in a wheelbarrow pushed by loyal friends.

Harvey Lobb: 1869 – 1958.
: President of the Blue Ribbon Oss Committee. A devoted Mayer and celebrated tenor of his day (sang 'I'm shy, Mary Ellen', at concert round Maypole, 1928).

Edgar C. Williams: 1971 – 1954.
: Another Maying fanatic, who would forsake his newsagent's shop regularly pre-1914 on May Days. His 1903 Broadsheet was the last to contain the full words, including the old Day Song. First President of Peace Oss Committee.

Thomas Henry Williams: 1884 – 1971.
: A keen historian of Padstow affairs, and President of Blue Ribbon Committee. Gave numerous lectures on the history and development of the Obby Oss. Was in South Africa in 1912 when exiles from Padstow made and danced before an Obby Oss, the highlight of a festival held by the Capetown Cornish Association.

Pat O'Keefe: Born 1929.
: Treasurer of Blue Ribbon Oss party from 1962 to 1976. Outspoken critic of the wrong kind of publicity for May Day at Padstow. Recently made history by telling the television teams and hippies they were not wanted.

Charlie Bate, 1916-1977.
: Inveterate Mayer and accordionist, has made a national name in the world of folk-song. A great entertainer and member of Old Oss team.

6. THE FUTURE

The whole story of the Padstow and its May Day has been one of continuing evolution and enlargement of the proceedings, if it had not developed and changed it surely would have died.

It has lost its rain-charming tradition: Treator Pool is dried up, the Oss is no longer immersed in the Quay waters, (though the Blue Ribbon team take theirs to 'Obby Oss' slip) nor are spectators sprinkled as an invocation for rain on the crops. Some of the Song has dropped out of usage and it is very difficult to fit the 'forgotten' words to music. The fertility rite, in these days of population explosion, is no longer looked on with the same favour as of yore. We still bring home the May and strew our flowers, but in the Age of Conservation how much longer shall we be allowed to do this? A May Day with plastic flowers is a looming possibility. Modern publicity brings vast crowds, which impede the Mayers, tend to discourage dancing, and make it difficult for the singers to follow the leader's words. The night singing is more apt to begin in a general hubbub than the expectant silence of former years during which the church clock could be heard to strike twelve.

Yet the loyalty of Padstonians, and others who come year after year, to their Osses, is still unquestionable, and there seems no reason to think that, having survived so long into the age of television and modern technological civilisation, May Day at Padstow will now decline and be abandoned. Certainly that ubiquitous menace the motor car cannot compete in Padstow on this one Day - for then people take precedence and few vehicles venture into the town, a case of proud old tradition triumphing over innovation.

So these are the Padstow Obby Oss and May Day Festivities, as strong in spirit as ever: indeed, more so, many people would say. Long may they continue, never to be preserved and fossilized except, perhaps, in these pages.

BIBLIOGRAPHY

Albino, H. Arlbutt:	Journal of E.F.D.S.S., 1939 (for May Song). Cecil Sharp House.
Alford, Violet:	Some Hobby Horses of Great Britain, in Journal of English Folk Song and Dance Society, Vol.111 No.4, 1939.
	Hobby Horses, Encyclopaedia Britannica, 1967 ed.
	The Hobby Horse and Other Animal Masks, in Folklore (Journal of the Folklore Society) Vol.79. Summer 1968.
Banks, M.M.:	The Padstow May Day Festival. Folklore, Vol.49, 1938.
Baring—Gould, Rev. S.:	Article, The Padstow Hobby Horse (May Day), in illustrated London News of c.1889.
	Mss., Plymouth Public Library.
	Songs of the West, 1891.
" " and H. Fleetwood Sheppard:	A Garland of Country Song, 1895.
Berry, Claude:	Cornwall. Robert Hale, 1949.
Bewnans Meriasek	translated Whitley Stokes, 1872.
Bottrell, Wm.:	Hearthside Traditions and Stories of West Cornwall, 1870 & 1873.
Canny, M.A.:	Boats and Ships in Procession, Folklore Vol.49, June 1938.
Chambers, Sir E.K.:	The English Folk Play, 1933.
Cornish Guardian	Bodmin: (in Public Library) Reports, 1901 — 1970.
Courtney, M.A.:	Folklore Vol.4, 1888.
	Cornish Feasts and Folklore, Penzance, 1890. (Cornwall County Library).
Creswell, Beatrice F.:	The North Coast of Cornwall from Constantine Bay to Crackington Haven. Homeland Association, 1908.
Edmonds, R.:	The Land's End District, 1862.
Frazer, Sir J.G.:	The Golden Bough. Macmillan, 1890 onward.
Gallop, Rodney:	in Folklore Vol.58, March 1947.
Gilbert, C.S.:	Historical Survey of Cornwall, 1817.
Graves, Robert:	The White Goddess. Faber, 1961.
Gundry, Inglis:	Canow Kernow, Songs from Cornwall. Federation of Old Cornwall Societies, 1966.
Hall, Reg. and Plunkett, Mervyn:	Ethnic, Summer 1959.
Harding, Henry:	in Western Antiquary, August 1883.
Harlow, Alan:	Ritual and Magic in Folk Song: May Rites.
	English Dance and Song, (Pub. E.F.D.S.S.) Spring 1967.
Hind, Lewis C.:	Days in Cornwall. 1907.
Hitchens, Fortescue, and Drew, Samuel:	Parochial Survey of Cornwall, 1824.
Hone, William:	The Every Day Book or the Everlasting Calendar of Popular Amusements, 1826.
Hunt, Robert:	Popular Romances of the West of England, 1865.
Jevons, F.B.:	Plutarch's Romane Questions. Bibilotheque de Carabas, 1892.
Kennedy, Douglas Neil:	England's Dances, 1950.
	Morris Dances, Encyclopaedia Britannica, 1967.
Kille, H.W.:	West Country Hobby Horses and Cognate Customs.
	Somerset Arch. Nat. Hist. 1931.
	The Minehead Hobby Horse (pamphlet).
Lach—Szyrma, Rev. W.S.:	in Western Antiquary, Vol.10, 1890.
Maylem, Percy:	The Hooden Horse, an East Kent Custom.
	Canterbury, 1909.
Nance, R. Morton:	in Journal of Royal Institution of Cornwall, 1936 (Helston Furry).
O'Neill, John:	Night of the Gods. London, 1893.
Peter, Thurstan:	The Hobby Horse, in Journal of R.I.C. Vol.19, 1913.
Polwhele, Rev. R.:	History of Cornwall. 1803.
Scott, Sir Walter:	The Abbot. 1820.
Shakespeare, William:	Julius Caesar. Act One.
Sharp, Cecil, and Broadwood, Lucy:	Journal of Folk Song Society, Vol.5, 1916.
Spooner, B.C.:	The Padstow Hobby Horse. Folklore, Vol.69, March 1958.
Tonkin, Edgar:	Devon and Cornwall Notes and Queries. Oct. 1922.
Trevelyan, Marie:	Glimpses of Welsh Life and Character. 1893.
	Folk—Lore and Folk Stories of Wales.

Old Oss and Musicians 1971.
(Photo: David Hills)

The Old Oss 1976. (Photo: Ray Bishop)

CAUTION.

NOTICE is hereby given, to all who have fired Pistols, Guns, or have let off Fireworks, to the annoyance of the Inhabitants of Padstow.

That in an Act entitled the Highway Act, passed in the 5th and 6th of William the 4th, Cap 50, Section 72, is the following clause.

"Any person who shall *wilfully* play at any game on highways, to the annoyance of passengers; or make or assist in making any fire, or *wantonly fire off any Gun, Pistol*, or let *off any Firework whatever*, within *fifty feet of* the centre of any carriage or cart-way; shall *forfeit* for either of the aforesaid offences, *a sum not exceeding forty shillings*, above the damages thereby occassioned."

We the undersigned Inhabitants of Padstow, very much disapprove of the proceedings transacted on the first of May, and *Resolve* to use our influence in accordance with the above clause to suppress the same, by taking down the names of those who violate the law refered to, and lodging the complaint to the Magistracy of this district.

Dated at Padstow, April 22nd, 1837.

M Prideaux Brune,	Nathaniel Oliver, senr.	George Hicks,
Vernon Collins, Officiating Minister,	James Hawken, senr.	John Stribly
	John Geach, senr.	Nathaniel Brewer
Paul O. Oke,	John Geach, jun.	Thomas Oliver
William Rawe,	George Geach	James Hawken jun.
Silas H. Paddon, R. N.	Edward Parnall	Sampson Tallick
John D. Martyn,	Thomas Raw Brewer, Waywarden	Humphery Buchanan
Price Rawlings,		William Perry
John Hawken,	Elijah Nance	Richard Brewer
John Phillipps,	Benjamin Harvey	James Vivian
Philippa Withell,	William Harvey	Jane Williams
Thomas Avery,	Joseph B. Mant	William Brown
Edward Edwards,	Thomas Mitchell	William Duggua
William Reynolds	William Broad	Henry T. Hawkey
Lucy Best,	A. P. Broad	Henry Mitchell
M. Broad,	John Courtenay	Samuel T. Evans
Thomas Carter,	Thomas Elliott	Thomas Withell
William Allport,	John Pearse, Treator,	Philippa Brewer
John Withell.	Martyn Richards, ditto,	Henry Harding
Francis Docton.	James Mason, Coll. H. M. C.	James Yeo
Nathaniel Oliver, Jun.	Joseph Martyn,	Joseph Williams
Jonathan W. Phillipps,	Richard B. Hellyar	Edwin Docton
Thomas Courtenay,	Matthew Trevan	John Raymond
John Sleeman	Henry Nance	Richard P. Griffin
Edward Stowers	Henry Elliott	William Hawken

DOCTON and SON, Letterpress and Copperplate Printers, PADSTOW

"The eyes of the LORD are in every place, beholding the evil and the good." Proverbs, 15 chapter, 3 verse.
"Why do the Heathen rage, and the People imagine a vain thing?" 2 Psalm, 1 verse.
"Let every one that nameth the name of CHRIST depart from iniquity." 2 Timothy, 2 chapter, part 19 verse.

Appendix A (see previous page)   The poster which ended the shooting. Before the passing of the 1835 Act against Firearms it was legal to fire off guns on the public highway (See Baring–Gould's reference to processions, p 19)   The gentry of Padstow were only too pleased to invoke the new Act, to end one of the features of May Day which they considered most distasteful and annoying, if not dangerous.

Appendix B. <u>May Rites.</u> A.L. Lloyd, in his book Folk Song in England (Laurence and Wishart, 1967) usefully discusses the background of fertility rites during the Middle Ages A Scottish priest is recorded as reviving the 'profane rites of Priapus' with a number of young girls, at Easter, 1282. The Church of the Middle Ages went through several periods of warring against such folk customs (of St. Augustine, p.12) and against minstrels who sang the common or bawdy folk–songs with their fertility symbols and references. 'All those improper gestures and disguises, the cross–dressed men–women, the ' man drunkards ' covered in animal skins or wearing bestial masks, the horse–dancers and the rest ..... were the regular target of eclesiastical anathema.' And again· 'The upholders of pagan beliefs and rituals in the villages were denounced as witches.' We have no evidence that such action on the part of the church was ever taken against Padstow people enjoying themselves on May Day; which is perhaps why the tradition has survived so strongly

In 1583 Phillip Stubbs, the Elizabethan puritan, was still railing against the same kind of thing in his Anatomie of Abuses . 'Against May, Whitsontide, or other time, all the yung men and maides, olde men and wives, run gadding over night to the woods, groves, hills and mountains, where they spend the night in pleasant pastimes; and in the morning they return, bringing with them birch and branches of trees to deck their assemblies withall.' Stubbs describes the bringing in and setting up of the May Pole 'with great veneration' and calls it a 'Stynking ydol.' 'And thus beeing reared up ... then they fall to daunce about it, like as the heathen people did at the dedication of the Idols.' He also records the defiling of maidens who spent the May Eve in the woods

Appendix C <u>The Bird in the Bush</u> Several folklorists, among them Simon Fury, have speculate on the possible connection between Padstow's Aunt Ursula Birdhood and the folk– imagery which appears in songs such as The Bird in the Bush. (The song often appears in collections, such as Baring–Gould's Songs of the West, under the title 'Three Maids Did a– Milking Go.')

In this folk song the bush represents the female sexual organ, and the bird, the male:

> 'Away to the green woods they went
> Away to the green woods they went
> And they tapped at the bush and the bird it did fly in
> And it flew just above her lily white knee.'

(James Reeves, the Idiom of the People, Heinemann 1958).

Baring–Gould's version, was collected at Lower Widecombe, and the metaphor is not so obvious; in fact this otherwise very Victorian guardian of morals allowed his version to be published without bowdlerisation.

> The verse 'Aunt Ursula Birdhood, she had an old yowe
> And she died in her own parc–O'

may therefore carry the connotation of an old maid dying without losing her virginity; something to be grieved over, as the tones of the dirge suggest. 'Aunt' used to be a common Cornish form of address to an elderly woman, not simply to a relative; and St. Ursula, after all, is the patron saint of virgins.

The question of the word Yowe raises further speculation. It has generally been spelled 'ewe' and may correspond to the ram's horns of the cuckolding theme (see p 16); but, Cornish 'yowynk' meaning either young or unmarried, may well have signified the virgin state of Aunt Ursula's vagina. The coincidental fact of the Birdhood family being well–known in Cornwall during the 18th and 19th centuries has possibly obscured the original meaning of these lines

PAST, PRESENT AND FUTURE
A Postscript

Looking back in 1999, it is clear that we owe the shape and pattern of our May Day festivities today, in greater measure than any other, to those young men who returned home after the Great War of 1914-18, determined to make this great day a worthy one for their town and towns-people. if we could return for an hour or two to the festivities of 1900 to 1910, we might well pity or smile at the mere handful of poor, drink-loving fishermen and their followers who each year brought out the Old Oss; and also at those who from time to time gallivanted out in various Blue Ribbon (or so-called Temperance) Osses.

The old photos we see of the Old Oss, bent and stiff with many coats of tar, the Blue Ribbons of its rival tattered, the poorly dressed musicians with triangle, side-drum, trombone, ukelele, concertina, all present a vastly different picture from that of today's well-organised, highly orchestrated teams of men and girls decked out in spanking whites. And if 'Bluey' England, William Henry Baker, 'Dolly' Denant, Trevethan Red, Dickie Brenton, Sammy Fielding, etc., could experience what we have made of their Day, would they smile - or be astounded, perhaps even appalled?

Today, in contrast to their own times, we are faced by what may be termed the Publicity Problem. Until 1970 or so, Padstow had never been loth to publicise its Great Day. During the 1930's, '40s and 50s, parties with both Osses even journeyed to the Royal Albert Hall in London to take part in National and International Folk Festivals - proud expeditions and great occasions, when the Padstow Obby Osses were given pride of place in the proceedings (see frontispiece). But television and the folk movement changed all that. Within a few years hordes of people were to descend on this little town: many behaved well and were genuinely interested, but others apparently cam here to drink themselves insensible, lying across our streets and quaysides, sleeping rough in Stile Field or in public shelters, and generally hampering the activities of the Osses, Teazers and followers.

A reaction was sure to follow, and in 1975 television camera crews were told they were not welcome. Since then few in Padstow have talked to radio or television interviewers or the press; no films or commercial recordings have been permitted. Drastic measures, which appear to have had the desired effect; recent years have been orderly in terms of crowds, yet some of the happiest from the point of view of the spectators and dancers. The advent of the May Bank Holiday (on the first Monday of the month) has had no detrimental effect on the festivities.

What other changes, for good or ill, would that stalwart band of pre-1914 Ossers see on our scene now? The actual singing of the May Song has hardly improved, perhaps because the massed drums and accordions drown the voices. Only six or seven verses of the Morning Song are in general sung during the day's festivities, with perhaps two or three more being heard during the Night Singing, from midnight on. (The night singing itself has been well organised over the past 20 years).

There is, of course, one well-tried way or reviving songs which are becoming disused or forgotten: actually teach them to the young. This has been successfully achieved with our own Padstow Carols, which otherwise might well have been lost to us some forty or forty--five years ago. Surely the schools could help by training Padstow children to sing their May Song, instead of apparently expecting them all to know it from birth. After all, there are 16 verses (apart from the refrain) in the Morning Song; it does take practice to remember them all. No one should be ashamed of consciously learning it, as all devoted folk-singers learn their songs.

A new development which might surprise our Edwardian celebrants is that of the Master of Ceremonies, resplendent in topper and tails: a touch of Helston Furry here perhaps. Not, I think, strictly traditional, though it is certainly picturesque. A feature lacking today, one which was usually evident in past years, is the May Lady: that jolly man-woman figure, the drag-queen of the May - Moll or Maid Marian. She was originally a Morris character, like the Oss himself, and the Teazer, or Fool, with his bladder on a stick. Our last May Lady was William Henry Thomas, who came out for many years in a green or pink dress, liberally painted and powdered, to dance with the Peace Oss and the Blue Ribbon Oss of post-war years. (See photo, p.26). The Revely brothers, Michael and Peter, have since, on occasions, played the part similarly dressed. During the 1920s and '30s the greatest Teazer (or, to give him his proper title, Dancer) of the century, J.H. MacOwen, also often appeared in skirts. (Once or twice he donned a kilt, to the disappointment of one venerable lady author, who recorded her regret in the pages of the Journal of the Folklore Society). Who, today, will carry on this centuries-old tradition? In Padstow we see men dressed as women in carnivals and pantomimes: why no longer on May Day?

As we go into the new millennium what can we expect of this, our own proud welcome to Summer? If we are as jealous now to protect and honour it, as we have been in the past, whether we are Ossers or spectators, folklorists or simple fun-loving Padstonians, we shall naturally want to see the best of our traditions kept up so that we can all enjoy them. But let us not be too narrow or parochial in our attitude. Padstow has, without exception, the liveliest and most unforgettable May Day ceremony anywhere, even if our Osses are not quite as unique as we like to think. (There are some 150 types of hobby horses appearing at various places and times in the year all over the globe). But when the Brenton Drum thumps into one's stomach and the great shout of "Oss, Oss! Whee Oss" goes up, we know that we are celebrating something older, more primitive and unspoiled, and much less self-conscious, than any contemporary religion or cult can offer. Should we - can we - keep it entirely to ourselves?

In the past the world has looked to Padstow to show it the way back to those happier, more innocent times when mankind was young. And surely Padstow still has something very valuable to tell our over-civilised, televised, computerised, bureaucratic world.

D.R.R.

April 1999